GO SCIENCE!

Motivation Progression Success

Berry Billingsley
Dave Mason
Nigel Saunders
Sian van der Welle

G9

Series editor:
Byron Dawson

BOOK **1**

www.heinemann.co.uk

✓ Free online support
✓ Useful weblinks
✓ 24 hour online ordering

01865 888118

Heinemann

D1647442

Contents

Chapter 1 Staying alive!

Chapter 2 Why are we different?

Chapter 3 What are things made of?

Key to how science works symbols

 investigation

 analysing data

 scientific models

 science in the news

 science and the world around us

Contents

How to use this book

Welcome to *Go Science!* We believe that learning about science, what scientists do and how science works should be fun. So we've packed in lots of amazing photos and illustrations, foul facts and interesting facts, as well as different types of exciting pages including 'setting the scene', focus on how science works and the best science lessons ever.

Here are the main types of pages in *Go Science!*

These are the 'setting the scene' pages. They tell you what you are going to be learning about in the chapter.

Here are some questions to get your brain warmed up before you get into the main lessons.

These photos give you some clues about what is coming up in the chapter. If you have the **LiveText CD-ROM**, you will be able to click on these photos and find out more.

Read about the illustration. If you have the **LiveText CD-ROM**, you will be able to click on 'hotspots' around the photo to discover more.

Questions in the text make sure you have understood what you have just read. They are colour coded and the levels are in brackets, so you know what level you're working at.

This is one of the main lessons. This box tells you what you will be learning about in the lesson.

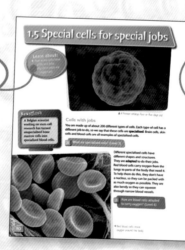
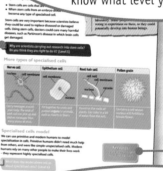

The keyword box lists all the keywords in a lesson. If you have the **LiveText CD-ROM** you can click on the glossary word and a pop-up box will give you its definition.

Key to question colours

 Level 3

 Level 5

 Level 4

 Level 6

In this 'focus on how science works' lesson you will look at some conservation issues.

Foul facts are about the 'yucky' parts of science.

Scientists don't just work in laboratories – they are involved in all sorts of interesting and exciting work.

There are levelled questions to make sure that you have understood what you have read.

You can read different people's views and make up your own mind.

We asked you what you liked most about science and many of you said it was the practicals, so we've included some best science lessons ever in the book.

Here's a step-by-step guide to what you will be doing in the practical.

At the end of the book, there are two science skills spreads that tell you about hazards and controlling risks in the laboratory, and how to plan and carry out investigations.

On the **LiveText CD-ROM**, there are five extension lessons that don't appear in this book, one for each chapter. These help you practise your scientific skills.

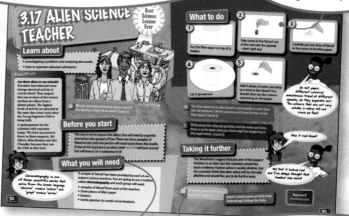

Here's a list of what equipment you will need.

At the end there are some questions for you to answer.

Introducing the *Go Science!* pupils

Ryan

Becca

Jasmine

Amber

Sam

Changing the world

We've been finding out what kinds of amazing gadgets we might have in the future.

Your toothbrush will inspect your teeth and tell you where to keep brushing.

There will be plasters that heal your skin as soon as you stick them on.

Your front door will recognise you and open automatically.

Your clothes will become waterproof in the rain and change colour if you tell them to.

The appliance of science

What will the future be like? Will you have a transporter? Or a cell-phone that runs on sugar? Will scientists ever invent a time machine?

Every day scientists find out more about how the world around us works. And whenever they make a major discovery, engineers make advances in technology that put this knowledge to practical use.

Around one hundred years ago, scientists discovered how to make electricity and send radio signals. Now we have mobile phones and televisions. Recently, scientists created some new materials. Engineers used these to make a shirt that plays music and a dress with fake flowers that open and close.

▲ This T-shirt is fitted with motion sensors and plays guitar chords as you move

A Name two inventions mentioned above which use radio signals and electricity. (Level 3)

Foul fact

Scientists have discovered that flies have glue on the hairs of their feet for added grip when they're upside down. If this glue turns out to be useful for us, you could one day see 'fly foot glue' in the shops.

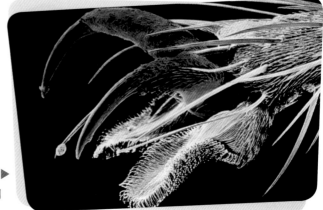

A fly's foot 'glues' ▶ it to the ceiling

How do scientists find things out?

Scientists spend months, even years, designing experiments and making observations.

There are different kinds of discoveries. Sometimes scientists see something new and unexpected. Scientists on a recent expedition to the swamps of South America discovered many new species, including a toad with fluorescent purple markings.

> **B** Why do you think scientists are interested in this species? (Level 4)

▲ A newly discovered species of toad

Looking for patterns and rules

Another thing scientists do is to look for patterns in nature. British scientist Robert Hooke refused to stop investigating, even to sleep. He noticed that if you add equal weights to a spring, it stretches by the same amount each time until it snaps. This observation became one of the laws of physics that we use today.

◀ Hardworking genius Robert Hooke investigated everything from living things to springs

Scientists use computer models to predict and explain the weather. These models are good but not perfectly accurate ▼

> **C** What did Robert Hooke find out about the way that a spring stretches? (Level 4)

Making models

Scientists create models that help explain why things happen as they do. Scientists have created models showing how air changes as it heats up and cools down. These models run inside supercomputers and they are used to predict and explain the weather.

> **D** Look at the ideas of models and predictions in the paragraph above, and explain why weather forecasters sometimes get the weather wrong. (Level 5)

Science and you

Leon is a speed skater. Whizzing round the track at about 90 km per hour, he's as fast as a car. Tricks of the trade include crouching down and holding one arm behind his back to reduce his air resistance.

Leon on speed skates ▲

Mark studied sports science at college and now trains a top football team. He says there's no beating the thrill of seeing one of his strikers score an incredible goal.

▼ Making predictions about the weather

Annie is a weather forecaster and she hates to get anything wrong. She reads a detailed forecast from the Met Office and then presents a weather spot on three local radio stations and one TV channel.

▲ Winning the match with skill and science

A Name three jobs mentioned above which require scientific knowledge. (Level 3)

What's the point of learning science? I don't want to be a scientist. I'm going to run a music studio – why do I need to know any science?

Scientific ideas

Long ago, a learned Greek called Aristotle taught his pupils that the job of the brain is to cool the blood. This is wrong, so how do we know that science books have their facts right today?

School science is built around well-tested scientific ideas. In science, you learn about collecting data, evaluating evidence and how scientists work.

Just like ice skating, football and the weather, there is a lot of science in sound mixing in a studio.

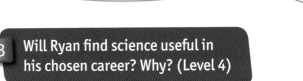

B Will Ryan find science useful in his chosen career? Why? (Level 4)

Why do science at school?

It says here that you need a basic training in science for all sorts of jobs. Sports coaches, clothes designers, windsurfers, zoo-keepers and plumbers all use science every day. Science is also fun! I like learning about how science affects the world around me.

▲ It takes a talented team of lighting and sound engineers to produce a good music concert

Science experiments

So, scientific ideas are useful in lots of jobs. But why do science students do experiments?

Experiments are great. You see things happening for yourself. That's more fun than just reading about them.

You build up your thinking skills because you have to work out what's going on – it's a brain workout!

Plus you learn scientific skills like observing and working safely – which I will need, since I'm going to be a famous scientist.

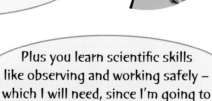

▲ Seeing science for yourself in a school science lab

 C Give three reasons why it is useful to do scientific experiments at school. (Level 5)

1.1 Living and growing

The world around us is full of tiny organisms. These are made of just a single cell which is too small for the naked eye to see.

All living things, including humans, are made of cells. But we aren't small – we are made of millions of cells. The photo on the right shows just a few of the red blood cells that can be found inside all of us.

A lot of microorganisms are made of just one cell and we need special ways to see them to find out why someone is ill.

- Make a list of the different types of living things you can think of.

- Name three of the seven life processes.

- Why can't we see organisms that are made of just one cell?

Coming up in this Chapter ...

 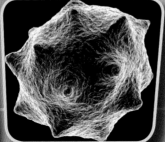 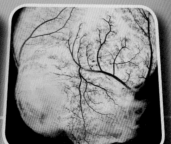 

1.2 Seeing cells

Sarah found some green slime in a lake. She wondered if it was living so she brought some home to show her brother Tim. 'We have to be careful – it may be poisonous algae,' he said.

After they washed their hands, Tim explained a very important theory in science called **cell theory**. Science has lots of big ideas, called theories.

Cells

Cell theory explains that all living things are made of **cells**. Scientists use microscopes to magnify cells as most of them are too small to see with the naked eye.

Tim showed Sarah how to look at the green slime with a microscope. She could see that it was actually a chain of little box-like cells.

> **A** Which of the following are made of cells? (Level 3)
>
> leaf   slug   2p coin   glass   leather   human
> plastic spoon   wood   brick   apple   rubber

> **B** Look at the photo of Sarah's slime. Do you think it is a living thing? Why? (Level 4)

Scientists use a thin specimen when they look at cells using a light microscope. If the specimen is not thin enough, the light cannot go through it.

▲ Sarah's slime magnified by a microscope

> **C** Why does the specimen on the microscope stage need to be thin if the cells are to be seen clearly? (Level 5)

Using a microscope

Scientists look down the **eyepiece lens**

They move the specimen into focus with the objective lens using the **focusing knob**

The specimen is mounted on a glass **slide**, covered with a thin glass **coverslip** and placed on a small platform called the stage

Light goes up through the specimen into the microscope

◄ How to use a light microscope

The eyepiece **magnification** multiplied by the objective lens magnification gives the total magnification of the microscope. For example, an eyepiece magnification of ×10 and an objective lens magnification of ×50 gives a total magnification of $10 \times 50 = 500$.

Interesting fact

The biggest cell is the Ostrich egg. The smallest is a bacterium called SAR11 (500,000 can fit into $1\,cm^3$ of sea water).

> **D** What magnification would you get with a microscope that had an eyepiece lens of magnification ×10 and an objective lens of magnification ×20? (Level 6)

▲ This scientist is looking at cells using a microscope

Electron microscopes

A German called Ernst Ruska invented the electron microscope in 1932. It uses streams of tiny particles called electrons instead of light. You can see the image on a screen instead of having to look down an eyepiece.

Keywords
cell, cell theory, coverslip, eyepiece lens, focusing knob, magnification, slide

A light microscope can magnify up to about 1,500 times, or ×1,500, but most school microscopes will only magnify to about ×400. Electron microscopes can magnify up to ×5,000,000! This allows scientists to see smaller cells and more detail inside cells.

1.3 What makes a cell?

Learn about:
- the parts of cells
- the differences between plant cells and animal cells

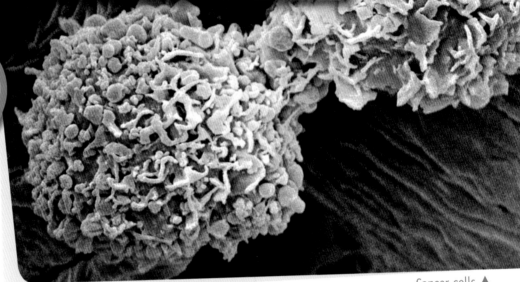

Cancer cells ▲

Cells multiplying out of control cause **cancer**. Doctors and other medical staff need to know all about cells if they are to cure diseases like cancer. Their knowledge comes from the information gathered by scientists over hundreds of years. They now know a lot about how cells work and why they sometimes don't work properly.

Sharing ideas

In 1873, two German scientists called Schleiden and Schwann were chatting over what they had found out about cells. They realised that plant and animal cells both had a **nucleus**. Then they used their imaginations to suggest that although cells have lots of differences, they all have the same basic structure.

When scientists share information or work together, they build a 'bigger' picture about the world and the way things happen.

> **A** Why do scientists learn as much about cells as they can? (Level 3)

An animal cell ▼

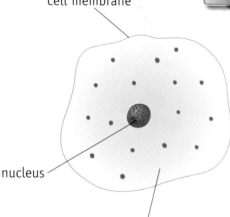

cell membrane

nucleus

cytoplasm

Inside cells

Cells come in all shapes and sizes. Most cells do not look like the 'typical' cells that you will find in most science books. But scientists have found that both animal and plant cells have some parts which are the same:

- nucleus – controls everything that happens inside the cell including multiplying to produce new cells

- **cell membrane** – lets substances such as water and dissolved gases into and out of the cell

- **cytoplasm** – where the chemical reactions that go on inside the cell happen.

Plant cells

Plant cells have more parts than animal cells:

- **cell wall** – a tough, supporting wall made from cellulose. It's like a cardboard box around the outside of the cell. It helps the cell keep its shape.
- **chloroplasts** – green bits inside most plant cells. They contain **chlorophyll**, which is a green substance that allows the plants to trap light so they can make food.
- **vacuole** – a space inside the cell filled with a watery liquid called **cell sap**. It helps to support the cell and keep its shape.

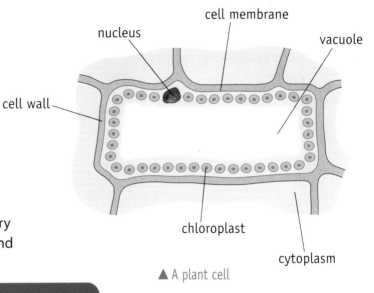

▲ A plant cell

B Write down one thing that plant cells have but animal cells don't have. (Level 4)

Scientists try to think of models for their ideas. You could try to make a model cell or just think about what a 'typical' cell will look like.

C Cancer is caused by cells multiplying out of control. What part of a cell do you think is going wrong? (Level 5)

D Look at the diagram of the mystery cell below. Do you think it is a plant or an animal cell? Give **three** reasons for your answer. (Level 6)

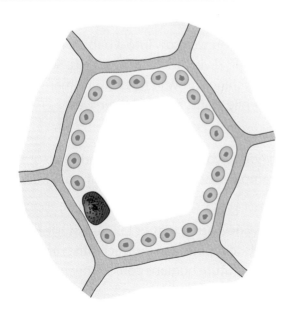

Science to the rescue

Scientists in Los Angeles have discovered that strawberry extract slows down cancer cell growth.

Keywords
cancer, cell membrane, cell sap, cell wall, chlorophyll, chloroplast, cytoplasm, nucleus, vacuole

1.4 How do we grow?

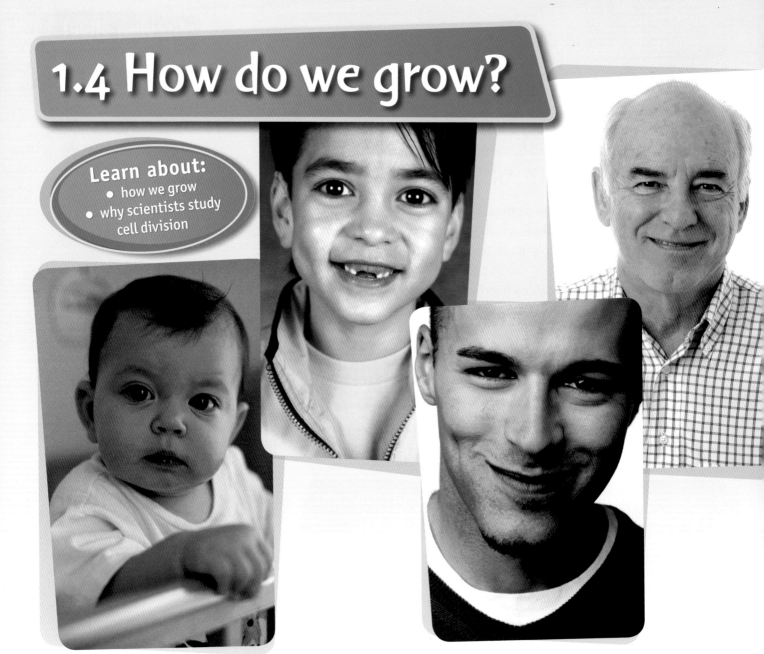

Learn about:
- how we grow
- why scientists study cell division

▲ We all grow up, but how do we do it?

We all start life as a single cell, then we grow into a baby, a child and finally an adult. We grow because our cells divide to make new cells. Scientists call this process **cell division**. All living things grow in this way. Humans stop growing when they become adults, while plants grow all their lives.

Running repairs

But your cells don't just divide so you can grow. The body also grows new cells to repair itself. For example, when you cut yourself, you grow new skin cells to repair the cut.

Some animals can even grow new arms, legs or tails. If a starfish loses one of its arms, it can grow new cells to replace the arm. Scientists are trying to find out how they do this, so in the future humans could grow new limbs if they lost them.

A Which parts of the body can a person easily replace? (Level 3)

Cell division

Sometimes scientists have to work like detectives. Cell division is a complicated process. Using a microscope, scientists could see all of the stages of cells dividing, but they had to work out the order in which things happened. They discovered that the nucleus always divides first.

When living things grow, cells divide over and over again until thousands of new cells are made.

How a cell divides and grows ▼

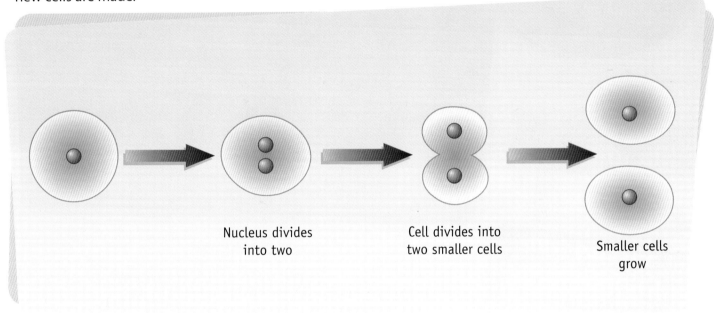

Nucleus divides into two

Cell divides into two smaller cells

Smaller cells grow

B What part of a cell divides first during cell division? (Level 4)

C State two reasons why our body cells divide. (Level 5)

Researching cell division

Scientists all over the world spend a lot of time trying to work out what controls cell division. They ask themselves these questions:

- How do cells know when to divide?
- Why do some cells divide but not others? For example, nerve cells don't divide at all.

People don't live forever. One of the reasons for this is that our cells stop being able to divide. In 1964 an American scientist called Leonard Hayflick discovered that most cells don't divide more than about 100 times. This means that our bodies stop being able to repair themselves when we get old.

D Cancer is caused by uncontrolled cell division. Explain why this type of cell division is so dangerous to our health. (Level 6)

Interesting fact

Problems such as cancer are caused because cells divide too often. These cells then grow into and destroy the tissues around them.

Keywords
cell division

1.5 All shapes and sizes

Learn about:
- how some cells have different jobs

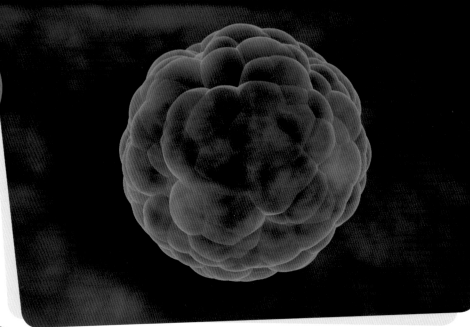

▲ A human embryo four or five days old

You are made up of about 200 different types of cells. Each type of cell is a different shape and size, and has a different job to do. Brain cells, skin cells and blood cells are all examples of cells with different jobs to do.

A Name five different cells you might have in you body. (Level 3)

Different cells have different shapes and structures. They are **adapted** to do their jobs. Red blood cells carry oxygen from the lungs to parts of the body that need it. To help them do this they don't have a nucleus, so they can be packed with as much oxygen as possible. They are also bendy so they can squeeze through narrow blood vessels.

B How are blood cells adapted to carry oxygen? (Level 4)

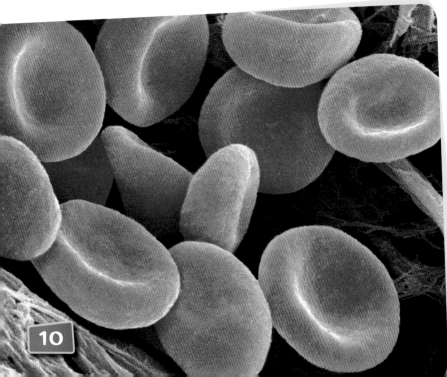

◄ Red blood cells move oxygen around the body

Stem cells

Your cells become adapted to do their jobs before you are born. Once a cell has become adapted, it can't change into another type of cell. For example, a skin cell can't change into a brain cell. **Stem cells** are cells that haven't become adapted to do a particular job, so they can become any type of cell.

Stem cells are very important because scientists believe they could be used to replace diseased or damaged cells. The most useful stem cells come from four- or five-day-old human **embryos**. An embryo is a ball of cells from which a baby grows. Using stem cells, doctors could cure many harmful diseases, such as Parkinson's disease in which brain cells get damaged.

Arguments over stem cell research

Stem cells are so important that scientists want to carry out more experiments on them. Scientists create embryos in the laboratory and then take stem cells from them. Some people think it is morally wrong to experiment on these embryos, as they could potentially develop into human beings.

C   Why are scientists carrying out research into stem cells? Do you think they are right to do it? (Level 5)

Different cells, different jobs

Type of cell	Nerve cell	Epithelium cell	Root hair cell	Pollen grain
What does it look like?	nucleus, cell membrane	cell membrane, nucleus	cell wall, cell membrane, nucleus, vacuole	
Structure	Very long, thin cells.	Small, fit together, can have hair-like structures called cilia.	Long, thin with a large surface area, found on the roots.	Small and light with 'sticky' ends so that it sticks onto a flower.
Function	Carry messages around your body very quickly (up to 300 km/h!). The ends of each cell can pick up and deliver messages from many places at once.	Covers the surfaces of parts of the body, e.g. the heart or lungs. The cilia help in the absorption and excretion of substances. In the lungs, the cilia wave together to move dirt out of the lungs.	Can take in a lot of water and minerals from the soil. The root hair cell gives the water more surface area to get into the cell.	The pollen cell joins with the female plant cell to make a new plant.

Keywords
adapted, embryo, stem cell

D   Describe what a skin cell might look like. How does this relate to its function? (Level 6)

1.6 COOKING UP A CELL

Learn about

- how cells can be modelled in different ways
- how to make a pizza model of a plant cell

▲ You can even use food to make models in science!

Class 7b are excited. Their school is holding a Year 7 cookery competition and the winning group will be taken out for lunch at a restaurant.

This looks great. We have to enter this competition.

Cookery competition!

Win a lunch at Bon Appetit restaurant with your cooking skills. But this is no ordinary cooking competition. You have to cook a delicious and accurate model of a cell.

We'll have to start thinking about the best way to model a cell then.

Before you start

Imagine that you are taking part in the Year 7 cooking competition. You need to organise yourselves into groups of four. In your groups, think of things you could cook to make models of plant and animal cells. For example, you could bake a cake with one cherry in it to represent an animal cell. Discuss all the ideas.

2D and 3D animal and plant cells ▼

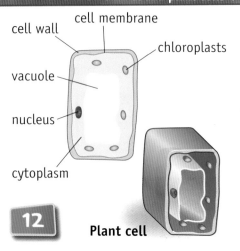

cell wall
cell membrane
chloroplasts
vacuole
nucleus
cytoplasm

Plant cell

cell membrane
nucleus
cytoplasm

Animal cell

A Which part of the cell would the cherry represent? (Level 3)

Write down in your groups your best idea for an animal cell and your best idea for a plant cell. (Remember, plant cells and animal cells are actually 3D but they are usually shown in science books as 2D.)

12

Each group takes it in turn to tell the other groups about their ideas. When all the groups have shared their ideas, the class then votes on the best idea for a plant cell and the best idea for an animal cell.

B Farah suggests a model of a naan bread baked with a dried apricot and some raisins inside it for an animal cell. Grace suggests a model of pineapple jelly with a strawberry in the middle. Which model do you think is best and why? (Level 4)

Making a pizza cell

Becca suggests making a pizza to model a plant cell. To make this model your teacher will take you to the Food Technology room. You will need for each group:

How to make a pizza cell ▼

- a ready-made pizza base
- orange cheese
- white cheese
- tomato puree
- 5 green olives
- one cherry tomato

What to do

1 Cut the pizza base into an oblong shape.

2 Squeeze the tube of tomato puree to make a line around the edge of the pizza.

3 Grate the orange cheese and pile around the edge of the pizza base.

4 Grate the white cheese and pile in the middle of the pizza base.

5 Put the olives around the edge on the orange cheese.

6 Put one cherry tomato on the orange cheese.

C Make a drawing of your pizza. Label the parts of your pizza to show what parts of the cell they represent. (Level 5)

D Evaluate the pizza model. What are the problems with this model? Suggest improvements you could make to it. (Level 6)

Interesting fact

A Belgian, Tom Waes, became the fastest person to eat a 12-inch pizza on 2nd December 2006. He ate his pizza in 2 minutes 19.91 seconds.

Voted a Best Lesson at St Saviour's and St Olave's School

1.7 Building blocks

Learn about:
- what tissues and organs are
- how scientists can create tissues and organs

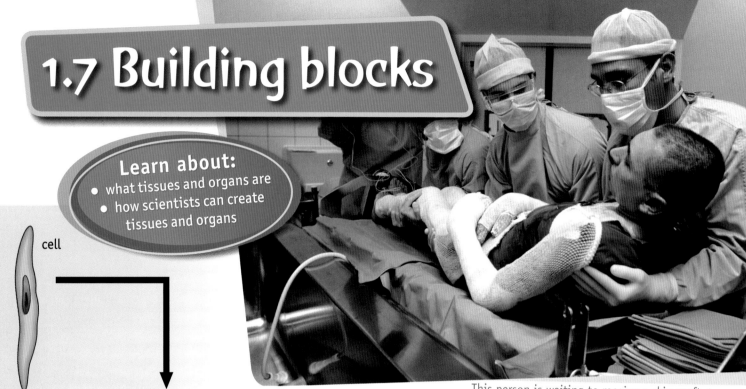

This person is waiting to receive a skin graft ▲

cell

muscle tissue

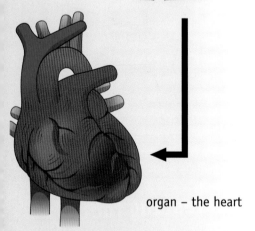

organ – the heart

▲ How cells, tissues and organs are organised

Onion skin tissue ▼

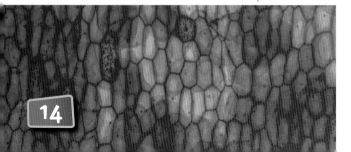

Simon has been burned in a fire. He is in hospital waiting for doctors to give him some new pieces of skin.

The skin is an **organ**. Organs are made of **tissues**, which are made of a collection of one type of cell. Skin is made up of skin tissue made from skin cells, nervous tissue is made from nerve cells, and muscle tissue is made from muscle cells. Different tissues carry out different jobs.

The heart is an organ and is made from tissues, such as muscle and nervous tissue.

A Explain what tissues are. (Level 3)

Some tissues and their jobs

Tissue	Job
bone tissue (animal)	to support the body
nervous tissue (animal)	to carry messages to all parts of the body
muscle tissue (animal)	to help us move
onion skin tissue (plant)	protects the leaves that make up an onion

Making tissues

Scientists can grow new tissues and organs in the laboratory. Scientists build three-dimensional structures and add tissue cells. Over several weeks the cells multiply and develop into tissues of the right shape. Skin tissue is quite easy to grow in this way. This is how Simon will get his new skin.

In 2006, scientists in the USA grew seven bladders from cells in the laboratory. These artificial bladders were then given to people with bladder problems. This was a breakthrough for people needing new organs or tissues.

Scientists are finding it hard to grow more complicated organs for transplanting into people to replace their damaged organs. A heart is very complicated and no-one has yet been able to grow heart muscle cells in the same way as bladder cells. But they believe that it will not be long before they can grow more complex organs. Only by scientists working together and sharing their ideas will this goal be achieved.

▲ Growing new bladders

B Why can scientists grow bladders but not hearts? (Level 4)

Making new plants

Plants are much better at replacing damaged tissues and organs than animals. Gardeners often take **cuttings** from plants. A cutting is just a little piece of stem and leaves. When the cutting is put into soil and given nutrients, it will grow roots, leaves and stem tissue, making a new plant.

Plant tissues can also be grown in a special jelly called a **culture medium**. This contains nutrients for the plant to grow. Scientists have developed ways of growing many thousands of plants from one original plant. They cut off small pieces of the stem and use the cells from it to grow new plants in glass bottles full of tissue culture medium.

Scientists at work

Scientists at University College London have created a living tissue which looks like pink jelly. It could be used to replace human tissues, such as skin tissue. It can be changed to become the type of tissue it is replacing.

▼ Taking a plant cutting

C Explain what a culture medium is. (Level 5)

D Explain whether receiving a pint of blood after an accident is an example of a tissue or an organ transplant. (Level 6)

Keyword
culture medium, cutting, tissue

1.8 Teamwork

Learn about:
- how organs work together to make an organ system
- how organ systems keep us alive

Sara having a check-up before her operation ▲

A life-saving operation

Only two weeks ago, 23-year old Sara Bertram was in a wheelchair and needed oxygen 24 hours a day. Sara suffers from cystic fibrosis, which is a disease that affects the lungs, and was losing her battle for life.

Today she is breathing easily for the first time in ten years. On Monday, surgeons took parts from her mother's and aunt's lungs and transplanted them into Sara's lungs. 'I can now live a normal life,' she happily told reporters.

Sara had an operation called an **organ transplant**. People have organ transplants when one of their organs doesn't work properly or stops working altogether. The new organ is given by another person.

You can give someone a kidney or part of your lung or liver, and still live normally, but other organs have to be taken from people after they die. People often carry donor cards to give permission for their organs to be given to someone else if they die.

A Why did Sara need new lungs? (Level 3)

Organ systems

The picture shows the different organs in your body. Organs work together in **organ systems** to do important jobs. Body systems are like teams. For example, your heart has a very important job pumping blood, but to do this it needs the blood and the blood vessels. The heart is part of the **circulatory system**.

The stomach and the intestine are part of the **digestive system**. This is where food is broken down to give you energy to move and grow. The brain is part of the **nervous system**, which carries messages around your body. In the **respiratory system**, the lungs are the organs you use when you breathe.

B Which organs work together in the digestive system? (Level 4)

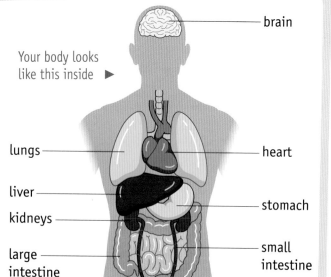

Your body looks like this inside ▶

- brain
- lungs
- heart
- liver
- stomach
- kidneys
- small intestine
- large intestine
- bladder

We can model how the body works by comparing it to a school with different teams of staff. The teachers, cleaners, office staff and teaching assistants do different jobs. They all work together to run the school.

C Doctors can now perform a triple transplant that includes the heart, lungs and liver. Suggest why this transplant is less likely to be as successful as a transplant involving a single organ, such as a kidney. (Level 5)

In the same way as in a school, all your organ systems work together to keep you alive and healthy. Models are a useful way of explaining how something works in a simple way.

Plants have organs too

The organs in a ▶ flowering plant

flower – for reproduction

stem – to hold the leaves and flowers in place

Life processes

The organ systems in plants and animals are very important because they allow the seven life processes to take place. The life processes are what every living thing needs to do to survive. There is a way to remember the seven life processes – think of Mrs Gren:

Movement	muscle and skeletal system
respiration	respiratory system
Sensitivity	nervous system
Growth	digestive system
reproduction	reproductive system
excretion	digestive, urinary and respiratory systems
nutrition	digestive system

leaf – to make the plant's food

roots – to anchor the plant and absorb water and minerals

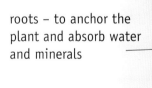

▲ Organisms need organ systems so they can move, feed and reproduce

Keywords
circulatory system, digestive system, nervous system, organ system, organ transplant, respiratory system

D Name two life processes that a rat and a plant can carry out, but an icicle and a toy car cannot. (Level 6)

1.9 Standing on the shoulders of giants

Learn about:
- how microscopes and our knowledge of cells have developed over time
- how scientists work together

▲ Van Leeuwenhoek's simple microscope (about 1670)

▲ Ernst Ruska with the electron microscope (1933)

◄ Zent Mayer's light microscope (1876)

During a trip to the Science Museum, class 7S were looking at the pictures in the History of Science section.

I can't understand what all the fuss is about with these old microscopes.

But if it wasn't for those old microscopes, we wouldn't know very much about the small things that make up our world. Just think about all the things we know about living cells that help doctors and researchers keep us healthy.

Yes, but scientists didn't find out the complicated things about cells from those microscopes.

Early discoveries

Van Leeuwenhoek and Hooke were discovering things at about the same time. Van Leeuwenhoek made really good lenses and made the first simple microscope, but Hooke made a more complicated type of microscope. If it hadn't been for Hooke's discovery of cells in cork tissue, Schwann and Schleiden wouldn't have discovered that cells had a nucleus.

Discoveries by early scientists have given us a greater knowledge and understanding of cells, which we use today. They were the 'giants' of science who have helped us find out more.

A Who made the first simple microscope? (Level 3)

Modern microscopes

Modern microscopes are much more powerful. Electron microscopes can magnify objects several million times. But living cells can't survive under the high vacuum inside electron microscopes – only light microscopes let us see living cells in action. The photos show some cells seen through an electron microscope.

B How many times wider is the egg than the sperm? (Level 4)

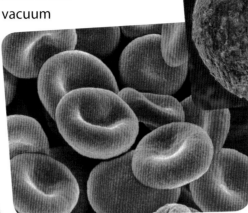

▲ Egg and sperm cells

▲ Red blood cells

Working together

Often, scientists work in teams to share the tasks involved in finding out new things. They need to make sure that they know all the important information that has already been discovered. Teamwork can also help them to evaluate one another's evidence so they can make suggestions for improvements.

▲ Scientists gather evidence and then share ideas in teams

Sometimes scientists swap ideas and discoveries in big meetings and conferences. They may write about what they have found out in papers, magazines, journals or on the internet. Publishing new ideas and discoveries is important for scientists. They want to get the credit for their work.

Scientists at work

The famous biologist, Charles Darwin, bought a new microscope to study barnacles in 1847. It magnified up to 1,300 times and cost £34!

C Describe different ways that scientists can tell people about their discoveries. (Level 5)

D Explain why it is valuable for scientists to work in teams. (Level 6)

Cutting edge

Modern technology, like email and the internet, has allowed scientists in different countries to work on the same problem while sharing results and ways of working. This means that news of breakthroughs travels much faster than it used to.

When scientists found a new way of studying the mysterious sugar molecules that are in every human cell which could lead to new cancer treatments, it was announced on the internet.

'Our findings represent real progress in this field of work and we believe that our methods will be used by scientists across the globe to push back the boundaries of international research.'

Professor John Gallagher, Cancer Research Campaign Research Centre

1.10 We want more pandas

Learn about:
● male and female reproductive systems

Panda in Beijing Zoo, China ▲

▲ Panda cubs born at Wolong National Nature Reserve, Sichuan, China

One day there might be no wild giant pandas left. To stop this happening, zoos need to breed more pandas which can be released back in the wild. These pandas can then breed other pandas.

Reproductive systems

To breed animals like the panda successfully, we need to know how their **reproductive systems** work. The reproductive system is an example of an organ system (see page 16). Most animals need a male and a female to reproduce. Their reproductive systems are very different.

● Males produce **sex cells** called **sperm**.
● Females produce sex cells called **eggs**.
● An egg and a sperm have to join together to make a baby.

Scientists use their knowledge about human reproductive systems to help people have babies.

A | What are the two types of sex cells produced by animals called? (Level 3)

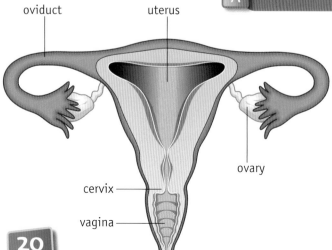

oviduct   uterus

ovary

cervix

vagina

The female reproductive system

The picture shows a human female reproductive system from the front. There are two organs called **ovaries** – one on each side. These are where the eggs are made.

Once a month, an egg leaves one of the ovaries and travels along the egg tube, or **oviduct**, to the **uterus**. The egg may meet sperm in the oviduct.

The uterus is where the baby develops. When the baby is ready to be born it is pushed through the **cervix**, which is a ring of muscle, and out through the **vagina**.

B What is the name of the organs that produce eggs? (Level 4)

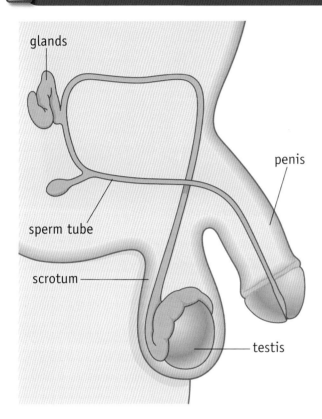

glands

penis

sperm tube

scrotum

testis

The male reproductive system

The picture shows a human male reproductive system from the side. There are two organs called **testes**. They produce the sperm.

The testes are held in the **scrotum**. This is a bag of skin which keeps the sperm at the right temperature.

The sperm pass along the **sperm tube** on their way from the testes out through the **penis**.

On their way through the sperm tube, the sperm pass two **glands**. These glands produce a liquid which is added to the sperm. The liquid and sperm mixture is called **semen**.

Interesting fact

A woman is born with all the egg cells that she will ever have. This is about 600 egg cells. A man makes about 10 million new sperm cells every day.

C About how long will it take a man to make 600 sperm cells? (Level 5)

Problems with reproductive systems

Sometimes there is a problem with part of a reproductive system that stops couples from having babies. This is called **infertility**.

The woman might not produce an egg every month. Or she might have blocked oviducts, so sperm cannot meet an egg. Some men don't produce many sperm, so it's less likely that a sperm will meet an egg.

D Suggest why some couples find it difficult for the woman to become pregnant. (Level 6)

Keywords

cervix, egg, gland, infertility, ovary, oviduct, penis, reproductive system, scrotum, semen, sex cell, sperm, sperm tube, testis, uterus, vagina

1.11 It takes two

Learn about:
- fertilisation
- how IVF can be used to help couples have babies
- how twins are produced

IVF can help couples to have children ▲

Newsflash

IVF can also help women who are over 50 to have babies. A woman over 50 is usually too old to produce eggs, so doctors use eggs from younger women.

Barry and Rachel have had successful **IVF** treatment. In the treatment, Rachel took drugs to make her produce lots of eggs. The doctor took the eggs from Rachel, took sperm from Barry and joined them together in a glass dish in a laboratory. The eggs were then put into Rachel's uterus and one of the eggs developed into a baby.

Babies born through IVF used to be called test-tube babies. The first test-tube baby, Louise Brown, was born in July 1978. Since then, about 30,000 test-tube babies have been born in the UK.

Fertilisation

The process of sperm joining with an egg is called **fertilisation**. Sperm and eggs are specialised sex cells.

A sperm and egg, not to scale ▼

Sperm are small and have long tails to help them swim towards an egg

Eggs are large, so they can store a lot of food for the developing baby

> **A** What is fertilisation? (Level 3)

Sperm cells travel from the testes through the sperm duct and out into the vagina

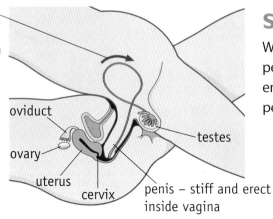

oviduct

ovary

uterus

cervix

testes

penis – stiff and erect inside vagina

Sexual intercourse

When a man and a woman make love, the man's penis becomes stiff. This makes it easy for the penis to enter the vagina. This is called **sexual intercourse**. The penis releases sperm into the vagina.

> **B** Explain what is meant by sexual intercourse. (Level 4)

Sperm meets egg

The sperm swim up through the uterus towards the oviducts. If an oviduct has released an egg, then the sperm surround it. One of the sperm burrows into the egg. The nucleus of the sperm and the nucleus of the egg join together. All the rest of the sperm eventually die.

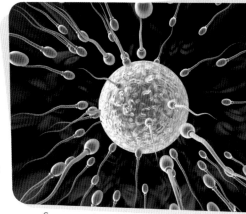

Sperm trying to fertilise an egg ▲

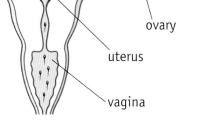

2 The egg passes along the oviduct

3 A sperm meets the egg in the oviduct and fertilises it

4 The fertilised egg passes along the oviduct to the uterus

1 An egg is released into the oviduct. Sperm are released into the vagina during sexual intercourse. They swim up through the uterus

ovary

oviduct

uterus

vagina

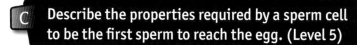

C Describe the properties required by a sperm cell to be the first sperm to reach the egg. (Level 5)

Twins

Occasionally a fertilised egg splits into two. As a result, **identical twins** will be born. Sometimes a woman produces more than one egg at a time. If two eggs are then fertilised, she will have **non-identical twins**. Rarely, three babies are born at once (triplets) or even four (quadruplets).

During IVF treatment, doctors often put more than one fertilised egg into the woman's uterus to give a higher chance of one of the eggs becoming a baby. Twins, triplets and quadruplets are often born as a result of IVF treatment.

These twins are identical ▲

D Do you think it's a good idea for couples who have had IVF treatment to have twins, triplets or quadruplets? Explain your answer. (Level 6)

Keywords
fertilisation, identical twins, IVF, non-identical twins, sexual intercourse

1.12 A new life

Learn about:
- how a baby develops in the uterus
- how a baby is born

Babies can hear music before they are born ▲

Scientists at work

Over the last 10 years, lots of experiments have been carried out which show that fetuses can hear sounds like music and doorbells.

- All babies start life as a fertilised egg. This divides to become an embryo, which is a ball of cells.
- By the time it is nine weeks old, the embryo is about 3–4 cm long and is called a **fetus**.
- It develops in its mother's uterus and is protected by floating in a bag of liquid. This liquid is called **amniotic fluid**.

A Where does the baby develop in its mother's body? (Level 3)

Scientists are discovering new things all the time about how fetuses develop. They used to think that fetuses were blind and deaf, with no sense of smell or taste. Now they think that fetuses can smell and taste.

Inside the uterus

The fetus needs food and oxygen, but it can't eat or breathe in the uterus. It gets its nutrients and oxygen from its mother's blood. The blood of the mother and the fetus never mix, but many substances cross from one to the other.

Part of the fetus is attached to the wall of the uterus. This is called the **placenta**. The placenta and the rest of the fetus are joined by the **umbilical cord**. As well as food and oxygen, harmful substances such as alcohol, drugs and chemicals from cigarette smoke can pass through the placenta into the blood of the fetus. This is why it is important for pregnant women not to smoke or drink alcohol.

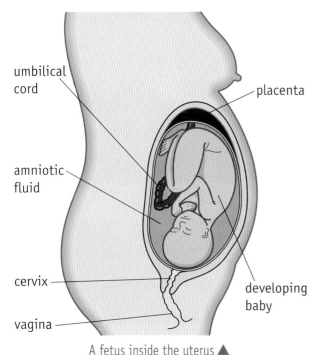

umbilical cord

placenta

amniotic fluid

cervix

vagina

developing baby

A fetus inside the uterus ▲

B What is the job of the placenta? (Level 4)

Amniocentesis

Doctors can check whether a fetus has **Down's syndrome** by taking a sample of amniotic fluid from around the baby. They use a hollow needle pushed through the mother's abdomen to collect the fluid. This test is called an **amniocentesis**.

About 1 in 100 babies die after an amniocentesis. As well as deciding whether to have the test, a mother also has to decide whether she wants to keep the baby if there is something wrong with it.

C Explain why a test where 1 in 100 babies tested will die is carried out on pregnant mothers. (Level 5)

Being born

After nine months, the fetus is ready to be born. The baby is pushed out of the uterus through the vagina.

Sometimes babies are born too early. They are called **premature** babies. They have to be looked after in a special-care baby unit, as they have problems breathing and sucking. Scientific advances now mean that babies as young as 23 weeks can be kept alive in **incubators**. An incubator is an artificial uterus. But such babies can be mentally or physically disabled, so some people don't think that they should be kept alive.

▲ A person with Down's syndrome usually has learning difficulties and can have heart problems

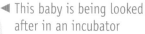

◄ This baby is being looked after in an incubator

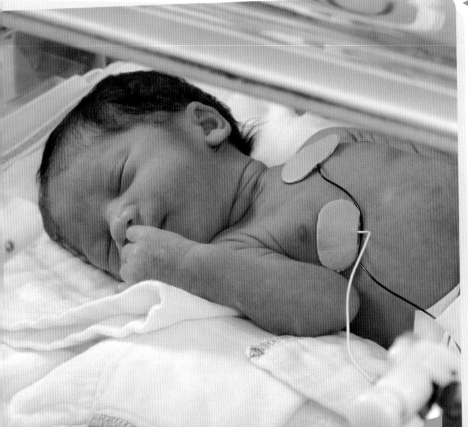

D Describe the features of an incubator that are needed to keep a premature baby alive. (Level 6)

Keywords
amniocentesis, amniotic fluid, Down's syndrome, fetus, incubator, placenta, premature, umbilical cord

1.13 Growing up

Growing up means many changes ▲

Learn about:
- what happens during puberty
- what menstruation is

When you grow up, your body goes through lots of changes, making you able to have babies. This is called **adolescence** and the changes to your body are called **puberty**.

Changes

Puberty is caused by chemicals called **hormones**. Boys' testes make the male sex hormone **testosterone**. Girls' ovaries make the female sex hormone **oestrogen**.

Puberty isn't just one change – it's a whole sequence of changes. They don't all start at the same age and they're not always in the same order. Girls usually start to change at least a year before boys. Some of the changes are obvious, like growing body hair. Others are less obvious, such as changes in emotions and behaviour.

Interesting fact

The word hormone comes from the Greek word 'hormon' which means 'to stir up'.

A	What causes puberty? (Level 3)

B	Describe **two** changes at puberty for boys, and **two** for girls. (Level 4)

How boys and girls change at puberty ▼

Changes in boys	Changes in girls
sudden increase in height (growth spurt)	sudden increase in height (growth spurt)
hair starts to grow on body, including pubic hair	hair starts to grow on body, including pubic hair
voice deepens	breasts grow
testes start to make sperm and hormones	ovaries start to release eggs and make hormones
shoulders broaden	hips widen
sexual organs get bigger	periods start

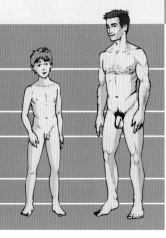

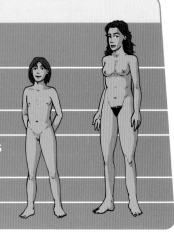

> Dear Sally
> Why am I different? My friends in school are all wearing bras and most of them have started their periods. Not much has happened to me yet! I've only grown a bit of pubic hair and my breasts aren't doing much. I'm nearly 13 years old and taller than most of them. Please help.
>
> Amber

Menstruation

During puberty, girls begin their **periods**. The scientific name is **menstruation**. The changes that happen to a girl's body between one period and the next are called the **menstrual cycle**. The menstrual cycle is controlled by female sex hormones.

An ovary releases an egg about 14 days before the next period. This is called **ovulation**. It happens when the uterus lining is most ready for an egg. If the egg isn't fertilised, the uterus lining breaks down. Cells and some blood flow out through the vagina. This is the menstrual period. After the period, the uterus lining is built up again ready for the next egg. If an egg does get fertilised, the girl's periods stop while she is pregnant.

C What happens to the uterus lining if the egg isn't fertilised? (Level 5)

Controlling fertility

Scientists can use artificial hormones to control fertility. Many women take the **contraceptive pill,** which contains hormones. The pill works by stopping the ovaries releasing eggs. Members of some religions, including some Roman Catholics, are against this practice.

Taking the pill can lead to health problems. Some women gain weight, get headaches or feel sick. Blood pressure can increase and blood clots may even develop. There is a higher risk of breast cancer. A woman has to weigh up the risk of getting pregnant against the health risks of taking the pill.

What happens during the menstrual cycle ▼

day 1 period starts (usually lasts 4-6 days)

day 6 uterus lining starts to thicken again

if egg not fertilised

day 14 egg released (ovulation)

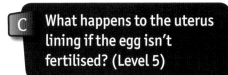

Keywords
adolescence, contraceptive pill, hormone, menstrual cycle, menstruation, oestrogen, ovulation, period, puberty, testosterone

D Describe the advantages and disadvantages for women of taking the contraceptive pill. (Level 6)

1.14 Finding patterns in data

Learn about:
- finding patterns in data
- gestation periods in animals

Wildebeest with newborn calf ▲

Zookeeper Noah is checking on one of the wildebeest as she gives birth.

'Generally, bigger animals have longer gestation periods – that's the scientific name for the time from fertilisation to birth. Wildebeest are pregnant for about 270 days,' says Noah.

Interesting fact

After a gestation period of one year, a female blue whale gives birth to a calf that averages 7 metres in length and weighs about 2 tonnes.

Looking for patterns

The table shows the gestation periods of different animals. The animals are in order of size. You can see a pattern in the data – the bigger the animal, the longer it takes to develop before it is born.

Gestation periods of different animals	
Animal	**Gestation period (days)**
mouse	21
squirrel	30
human	265
camel	355

A | What is the gestation period of a squirrel? (Level 3)

Exceptions to the rule

Scientists are always looking for patterns in their observations, but there are always exceptions. The table shows the average size of an animal and its gestation period.

Gestation periods and sizes of animals

Animal	Gestation period (days)	Average mass (kg)
moose	245	726
human	265	73
giraffe	425	1900
elephant	645	7000

B Usually the larger the animal, the longer is the gestation period. Which animal in the table doesn't fit this pattern? (Level 4)

Making observations

Sometimes scientists can't find out something by doing experiments, so they have to make lots of observations of things that change, which are called variables. Then they look for the patterns behind the observations and suggest reasons for them.

All animals release eggs. Fish and birds lay their eggs, which hatch. One group of animals, called mammals, give birth to live young. Humans don't release many eggs compared to fish – normally only one egg at a time, while fish such as salmon may release thousands.

Reproduction variables

Variable	Salmon	Blackbird	Human
internal fertilisation	no	yes	yes
young born alive	no	no	yes
good parents	no	yes	yes
number of eggs released at one time	1000	5	1

The table shows that animals that release the fewest eggs:

- have internal fertilisation – this means that eggs are fertilised inside the mother's body
- give birth to live young
- are good parents.

Scientists suggest that this is because internal fertilisation makes an egg more likely to be fertilised. Giving birth to live young and being good parents mean that babies are more likely to survive to become adults.

Salmon eggs are much less likely to become fertilised and baby salmon are less likely to survive, so salmon need to release more eggs.

C Why do fish release so many eggs? (Level 5)

▲ A female salmon can lay over 1000 eggs, here are just a few of them

D Suggest a pattern, other than eggs released, that can be found in nature. (Level 6)

1 Assess your progress

1.2 Seeing cells

1 What is the biggest cell in the animal world? (Level 3)

2 Complete the following sentence:
   All living things are made up of _____ . (Level 3)

3 What part of the microscope is turned to get a clear image of the specimen? (Level 4)

4 Why are microscope slides made of glass? (Level 5)

5 Hand lenses, light microscopes and electron microscopes can all be used to look at small objects.
   Which one would you use for magnifications of:
   a ×5; **b** ×100; **c** ×400; **d** ×10,000? (Level 6)

1.3 What makes a cell

1 Unscramble the letters to find the names of parts of a cell: **a** lemel cernbam; **b** ovaluce; **c** uncluse (Level 3)

2 What is the name of the green substance inside chloroplasts? What do plant cells use it for? (Level 3)

3 What **three** things are found in both plant and animal cells? (Level 4)

4 Why are models useful when describing cells? (Level 5)

5 Some organisms are made up of just a single cell. Describe the jobs that the single cell must do to keep the organism alive. (Level 6)

1.4 How do we grow?

1 Name a type of cell that does not divide. (Level 3)

2 State the difference between growth in humans and growth in plants. (Level 3)

3 If one cell divides six times, how many cells will be produced? (Level 4)

4 At what point in the cell's cycle of division do cells grow in size? (Level 5)

5 Explain why it is important for scientists to find out more about cell division. (Level 6)

1.5 All shapes and sizes

1 Why do cells have different shapes and structures? (Level 3)

2 Name **three** cells that are adapted to do different jobs. (Level 3)

3 Suggest **one** use for stem cells. (Level 4)

4 Explain why stem cells are different from normal body cells. (Level 5)

5 Sickle cells are red blood cells that stick together and become stiff after they deliver oxygen. Explain why a sickle cell is less efficient at carrying oxygen around the body than a normal red blood cell. (Level 6)

1.7 Building blocks

1 What sort of cells make up muscle tissue? (Level 3)

2 Name one tissue in a human and **one** tissue in a plant. What are their jobs? (Level 3)

3 Why is the heart described as an organ? (Level 4)

4 **a** Which type of cells are quite easy to grow in the lab? **b** How can they be used? **(Level 5)**

5 Suggest a reason why it is important for scientists to develop new ways of growing tissues in the lab. (Level 6)

1.8 Teamwork

1 Why is there a waiting list for heart, lung, liver and kidney transplants? (Level 3)

2 Match up the organ with the correct organ sysyem it is part of
   heart   stomach   lungs
   digestive system   circulatory system   nervous system
   (Level 3)

3 Zac235 is a robot. He looks exactly like Zac Jones, the astronaut he was modelled on. Make a list of the life processes that Zac235 is unable to do (Level 4)

4 Put the following words in the correct order, starting with the simplest structure first. (Level 5)
   organ   system   tissue   organ   cell

5 Do you think that the organisation of a school is a good model for organs working in a system? Why **or** why not? Give you reasons. (Level 6)

1.9 Standing on the shoulders of giants

1 Give **two** ways in which scientists share their discoveries, thoughts and ideas. (Level 3)

2 From the information on pages 18 and 19, arrange the following scientists in chronological order: Darwin, Ruska, Hooke, van Leeuwenhoek. (Level 4)

3 Suggest why science cannot give exact answers to some of society's questions, such as 'Is there a God?'. (Level 5)

4 Do you think that the cells in the photos on page 19 have been viewed using a light microscope or an electron microscope? Why? (Level 6)

1.10 We want more pandas

1 Name **three** parts of the female reproductive system. (Level 3)

2 Unscramble the letters to find the parts of the male reproductive system: **a** snipe; **b** stites; **c** morctus; **d** sremp bute (Level 3)

3 What is the job of the penis in reproduction? (Level 4)

4 Why do you think males produce a lot of sperm? (Level 5)

5 Which cells will be the oldest: sperm cells from a 30-year-old man or egg cells from a 20-year-old woman? Explain your answer. (Level 6)

1.11 It takes two

1 Explain why a sperm cell has a long tail. (Level 3)

2 Explain why the penis becomes stiff before sexual intercourse. (Level 3)

3 What happens during IVF treatment? (Level 5)

4 Arrange the following parts of the female body in the order that the sperm passes through: uterus, cervix, oviduct, vagina. (Level 5)

5 In what way is the sperm specialised to allow it to get to the egg? (Level 6)

1.12 A new life

1 What is the job of the amniotic fluid? (Level 3)

2 How long does a human pregnancy last? (Level 3)

3 How is a fetus attached to its mother's uterus? Explain why it is attached. (Level 4)

4 Describe the possible problems faced by parents who have a premature baby. (Level 5)

5 Why is it not a good idea for pregnant women to smoke or take drugs? (Level 6)

1.13 Growing up

1 What is the name for the bodily changes that happen during adolescence? (Level 3)

2 What controls the menstrual cycle? (Level 3)

3 There are several visible physical changes that happen during puberty. What is a less obvious change that happens during puberty? (Level 4)

4 Why does the wall of the uterus thicken during the menstrual cycle? (Level 5)

5 What might cause a girl's periods to stop? (Level 6)

1.14 Finding patterns in data

1 What do we call the time taken for a baby animal to develop inside its mother's uterus? (Level 3)

2 Why do human females release only one egg at a time? (Level 4)

3 Explain the difference between observations and variables. (Level 5)

4 Why do scientists feel that it is important to look for patterns in data? (Level 6)

2.1 Digging up the past

Mary Anning was born in Lyme Regis on the south coast of England in 1799. She and her family found lots of fossils in the cliffs near where they lived. Mary and her brother were the first people to discover an ichthyosaur dinosaur skeleton in 1812.

The fossils Mary collected were like the missing pieces of a jigsaw. Each fossil she found allowed other scientists to begin to classify extinct animals and plants, and build up a picture of what life was like millions of years ago.

Sadly, Mary was almost forgotten after her death in 1847. Scientists at the time did not think that a woman could have such an important influence on their subject.

- What does it mean if we say an animal is extinct?

- Where did Mary Anning find the fossils?

- Why are fossils important to scientists?

Coming up in this Chapter ...

2.2 The same but different

Learn about:
- how living things have similarities and differences in their features
- what a species is
- how some features are inherited and some are not

Fit for the job ▲

The dogs in the photo are all working dogs. They have been bred to have the **features** which allow them to carry out their jobs. The police use German shepherd dogs to help them find criminals. Labradors are often used as guide dogs.

The same species

Although these dogs are all different, they also have lots of features in common. Scientists say that they belong to the same **species**. A species is a group of animals or plants that can breed with each other to produce **fertile** offspring. This means that the offspring can reproduce.

Scientists group plants and animals into species because they are so varied. It makes studying them easier. Scientists look for special features to decide whether organisms belong together in the same species.

▲ Pedigree dogs are bred only with the same breed so that owners can be sure what features they will have. Some people think this isn't a very good idea because some of the dogs develop problems with their health

A Explain what a species is. (Level 3)

Having things in common

Members of the same species are never quite identical, even if they are twins. Look at Stewart, Michael and Yasmine on the next page. They are all human beings and belong to the same species.

Interesting fact

Some dogs have been bred to have no hair, such as the Mexican hairless dog.

These students have some features in common. They also have some features which are different. For example, Yasmine and Michael have different hair and eye colours, while twins Stewart and Michael are good at different subjects.

Some of their features are **inherited** from their parents, such as hair colour. Others are due to their **environment**, such as having pierced ears or tattoos. Usually the environment and inheritance work together to give a living thing its features.

B | Twins Stewart and Michael both have brown eyes. Do you think this feature is inherited or due to their environment? (Level 4)

Breaking the rules

Safari park announces the birth of a zebroid!

Zebroids are zebra crosses. A zebra/donkey cross or zonkey was born last night at Africa World Safari Park. If a zebra reproduces with a pony the result is a zony.

Some very similar species can breed together. Tigers and lions can reproduce to produce a liger, if the male is a lion and the female a tiger, or a tigon, if the male is a tiger and the female a lion. Ligers are the world's largest cats, but tigons tend to be small. Male ligers and tigons are **sterile**. This means they cannot reproduce.

This is a liger ▼

My name is Stewart. I am really good at English.

My name is Michael. I am Stewart's identical twin. I am good at Science.

My name is Yasmine. I am in the netball team.

▲ Stewart, Michael and Yasmine are in the same class for science

C | Horses and zebras are not the same species but they can breed together to produce offspring. How is this possible? (Level 5)

D | Mules are the result of a horse and a donkey breeding together. This is the only way of producing a mule. Why is it not possible to breed a mule from two parent mules? (Level 6)

Keywords
environment, feature, fertile, inherited, species, sterile

35

2.3 Sort it out!

Learn about:
- why living things are classified
- how organisms are named
- how classification has changed

There are millions of different species on Earth ▲

It is hard to guess exactly how many different species exist at the moment on Earth. There are many that we have not yet discovered. The total number is likely to be between 13 and 14 million but we have only given about 1¾ million different species scientific names.

Interesting fact

Insects make up two-thirds of all living things.

A Why is it difficult to say exactly how many different species exist on Earth? (Level 3)

Why classify living things?

For a very long time scientists have known that when we study living things it helps to put them into groups with other very similar organisms.

We call this **classification** and it is one way of thinking about plants and animals.

If we know a lot about one animal or plant, we can use this information to help us study another one in the same group because they have similar features.

B Why is it a good idea to put similar, closely related, living things in the same groups when we classify them? (Level 4)

◄ Knowing about other insects can help us study this one

Naming things

Carolus Linnaeus was a Swedish botanist and a medical doctor. He wrote 180 books on plants. In 1735 he wrote *Systema Naturae* in which he explained a way of classifying all living things. This is the system that we still use today.

In this system, each organism has two Latin names. You will often see these names on information labels in museums or zoos. They are used by scientists all over the world. This is so they can share information about living things without being confused about which organism they are talking about. Because there are two parts to the name, it is called the 'two name' or **binomial system**.

C   **Why is it a good idea to have a standard system of naming living things? (Level 5)**

Ways of classifying living things

Aristotle was a Greek philosopher who lived about 2,350 years ago. He was the first person to classify living things. He said that things that moved were animals, and things that were green were plants.

> I don't think Aristotle was right. This frog is green and it can move.

John Hogg, in the nineteenth century, classified living things as animals, plants and microbes. He said that microbes were any living things that could only be seen with a microscope.

At the moment, scientists put living organisms into five **kingdoms**. Every species belongs to one of them. Two of these kingdoms are animals and plants.

In the future, scientists may use a different way of classifying. Some scientists have already suggested a new way of classifying living things by looking at what **genes** they have. This is an example of how science changes.

Tiger
Panthera tigris

▲ We still use the system of classification that Linnaeus invented

Scientists at work

Scientists have named 375,000 species of plants. Each year they find and name more species.

D   What might cause scientists to change their minds about how to classify living things? (Level 6)

Keywords
binomial system, classification, gene, kingdom

37

2.4 Spineless!

Learn about:
- why invertebrates are important
- how invertebrates can be classified
- how we can protect invertebrates

Aborigines in Australia eat these witchitty grubs ▲

Invertebrates may be small but they are very important living things. Sir David Attenborough, a famous naturalist, has said:

> If we and the rest of the back-boned animals were to disappear overnight, the rest of the world would get on pretty well. But, if the invertebrates were to disappear, the world's ecosystems would collapse.

Invertebrates are animals without backbones. At least 90% of all animal species on Earth are invertebrates. There are more than 40,000 species in the UK alone.

Why are invertebrates important?

Invertebrates are important as food. They are eaten by many birds and mammals. For example, baleen whales eat tiny shrimp called krill. Humans can eat some types of invertebrates too. Invertebrates also feed on other invertebrates, so they can help to control garden pests such as aphids.

Science to the rescue

Rachel is a nurse. She says, 'Once, a patient had a wound that just wouldn't heal, and I put maggots on it. It was very satisfying picking off the maggots a few days later when they had grown big and fat. The wound had healed beautifully.'

A (i) Why are invertebrates important to larger animals such as mammals and birds? (ii) Explain how they help to control garden pests. (Level 3)

Invertebrates have other uses. Maggots can be used by doctors to clean infected wounds. They put them on the wound for a few days under a bandage. The maggots eat any rotting flesh leaving the wound healthy.

Sorting them out

Mrs Reid has organised for a project officer from Buglife, the Invertebrate **Conservation** Trust, to visit her Year 7 pupils. Conservation means trying to protect animals or plants in a habitat. The project officer explains how invertebrates are classified into seven groups and shows the pupils some photos.

▼ Mollusc

Starfish ▲

Arthropod ▲

Segmented worm ▲

▲ Flatworm

Jellyfish ▲

Roundworm ▲

B Look at the seven invertebrate groups above. Which group has (i) a flattened body, (ii) a star-shaped body, (iii) a jellylike body? (Level 4)

C Megan has found a sea creature with a hard body and five arms. Jo says it is a brittlestar. Which invertebrate group does this creature belong to and how can Jo be sure? (Level 5)

Helping invertebrates

The project officer explains that bumblebees are important invertebrates. They are responsible for transferring pollen between flowers so that the flowers can make seeds. But they have been disappearing and the short-haired bumblebee has disappeared completely from the UK.

▲ Bumblebees help plants to reproduce

Interesting fact

Nearly 2000 species of insect are in danger of dying out in the next few years.

Scientists at Buglife are running a project called 'All of a Buzz' in London and Essex to encourage people to look for and count bees in their gardens. The scientists hope that if people have a better understanding of what bees need to live, then this will help the bees to survive.

D Farmers and gardeners often use chemical weed killers to remove unwanted plants. How might this reduce insect numbers? (Level 6)

Keywords
conservation, invertebrate

2.5 The bare bones about vertebrates

Birds

emu

Reptiles

rattlesnake

Fish

angel fish

Mammals

gorilla

Amphibians

tree frog

▲ The five vertebrate groups

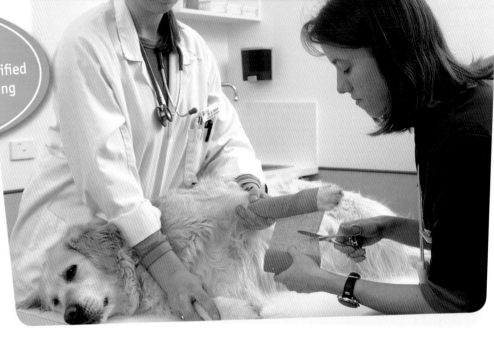

Tara's dog, Oscar, has been hit by a car. The dog is limping badly so she takes it to the vet. The vet takes an X-ray of Oscar's front leg. When the X-ray is ready, the vet shows it to Tara.

'The X-ray shows that one of Oscar's leg bones is broken. We'll need to put it in plaster and it will take several weeks to heal. Oscar won't be doing much running around for a while,' she says.

Dogs, like Oscar, are classified as **vertebrates**. This means they have a skeleton mostly made up of bone, and a backbone.

A Explain how vertebrates are different from invertebrates. (Level 3)

Vertebrate groups

All vertebrate animals have backbones and a bony skeleton. Because of this they are similar but, because they also have differences, scientists put them into five groups. The picture shows the five groups with an example of each type.

B Make a list of two other examples to fit into each group. (Level 4)

More about the groups

Mammals usually have bodies covered in hair. Their babies develop inside the mother's body and when they are born they are fed on milk from her mammary glands.

Young crocodiles can look after themselves as soon as they hatch ▼

Reptiles have dry scaly skins and lay eggs with leathery shells. Their young hatch from the eggs ready to feed and look after themselves. Reptiles live mostly on dry land.

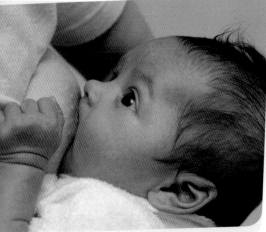
◀ Humans are also mammals

Amphibians lay their eggs in water, although they breathe air and live partly on land. They have smooth, damp skin.

Birds have bodies covered in feathers and most of them can fly. They lay eggs with hard shells. When their chicks hatch, the parents feed them and look after them.

Fish have scales and fins. All fish live in water and they lay their eggs there too. They breathe using gills.

C Why do fish produce very large numbers of young? (Level 5)

Foul fact

The most deadly creature on Earth is probably the tiny golden poison dart frog. One milligram of its poison is enough to kill 10,000 mice or 10–20 human beings.

The echidna problem

Echidnas are found in New Guinea and Australia. They are small with spines like hedgehogs. A female echidna lays one leathery egg. She puts this egg into a pouch on her body. When the baby, called a puggle, hatches, it sucks milk from milk patches inside the pouch.

So which vertebrate group does an echidna fit into? It is actually an egg-laying mammal. Scientists had to invent a new subgroup to classify echidnas. The subgroup is called the **monotremes**. The only other member of the subgroup is the duck-billed platypus.

D Think about the echidna. What features tell scientists that although it lays eggs it is still a mammal? (Level 6)

Keywords
amphibian, bird, fish, mammal, monotreme, reptile, vertebrate

Which group does the echidna belong to? ▼

41

2.6 Putting plants in their place

Learn about:
- how plants are different from animals
- how plants can be classified

All these are plants. But how do we know?

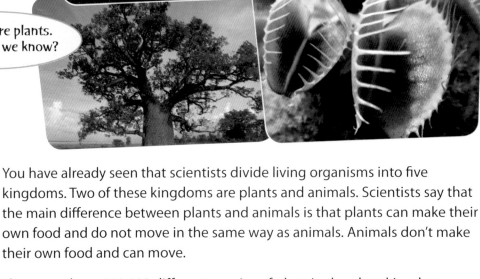

You have already seen that scientists divide living organisms into five kingdoms. Two of these kingdoms are plants and animals. Scientists say that the main difference between plants and animals is that plants can make their own food and do not move in the same way as animals. Animals don't make their own food and can move.

There are about 300,000 different species of plant in the plant kingdom. This is much smaller compared to the number of different animals.

A   What are the main differences between plants and animals? (Level 3)

Identifying plants

People come from all over the world to see the plants at Kew Gardens near London. Sometimes they bring plants to the experts at Kew and ask them what they are. Jasmine has found a strange plant growing in her garden. She has brought it to Kew.

Kew Gardens ▼

Foul fact

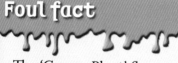

The 'Corpse Plant' flowers every four to ten years and smells like a rotting body. The smell attracts beetles and flesh flies which pollinate it.

'One way of classifying plants is by how they reproduce. Some plants make seeds and others don't. Plants that do make seeds can be classified as **flowering** or **non-flowering**. Conifers, for example, are non-flowering plants. They produce seeds but they develop inside cones rather than inside flowers,' explains the curator.

B Why are conifers classified as non-flowering plants? (Level 4)

The mystery plant

The curator takes a look at Jasmine's plant. 'Some flowering plants have narrow leaves. The flowers are usually small and not very interesting. Palms and grasses also have narrow leaves. Other flowering plants have broad leaves. Their flowers are often really colourful. Roses and buttercups have broad leaves.'

C Take a look at Jasmine's plant on the right. Describe what type of plant it is and why. (Level 5)

▲ Jasmine's plant

Classifying plants

Rona and Leo are on a school trip to a botanic garden. They take photos of different kinds of plants. Their photos are shown below. When they are back in the classroom, they classify the plants by dividing them into two groups.

Then they take one of the groups and divide it into two more groups. Rona and Leo repeat this process until all the plants are classified. They know that there are lots of ways of putting the plants into groups.

D (i) What two groups could Rona and Leo divide the six plants into first? (ii) Take the biggest group and explain how you could divide this group into two more groups. (Level 6)

Keywords
flowering plant, non-flowering plant

43

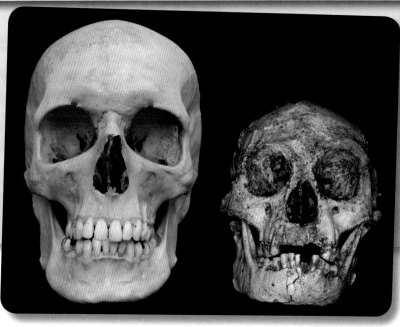

◀ Human skull (left) and 'Hobbit' skull (right)

Chris Stringer is Head of Human Origins at the Natural History Museum in London. The museum houses an enormous collection of plant and animal specimens. It has scientists who can help investigate unknown organisms.

Chris has been involved in discussions about the 'Hobbit' that was found in Indonesia in 2004.

Long-lost relative?

The 'Hobbit' was a 1 m high species that lived on Flores Island. Its skeleton was found in a cave on the island, surrounded by a lot of sophisticated stone tools. The scientists named it *Homo floresiensis*.

The skeleton is so small that at first scientists thought it was a child. But investigations showed that it was an adult female. The skeleton is about 18,000 years old. It has long arms, a small skull and a chimp-sized brain.

Chris Stringer has suggested that its long arms might show that the 'Hobbit' spent a lot of time in the trees. It lived on the island with Komodo dragons and dog-sized rats, so living in trees would have been a sensible way of life.

Scientists at work

Scientists hope to get genes from the 'Hobbit' skeleton so that they can see just how closely related to humans it really is.

A | Why did the scientists think at first that the 'Hobbit' skeleton was a child? (Level 3)

B | What was the main advantage of living in the trees? (Level 4)

A Komodo dragon ▶

Scientists sometimes disagree

Some scientists, including Henry Gee of *Nature* magazine, suggest that some 'Hobbits' could still exist today. Flores islanders tell stories and have legends about small people living on the island up to 100 years ago. They call the little people Ebu Gogo.

Other scientists do not agree. They think that the 'Hobbit' died out 12,000 years ago when a volcanic eruption killed off most of Flores Island's wildlife.

Yet, there are dense, unexplored forests in Indonesia where small human-like creatures could live undiscovered…

> **C** The Indonesian forest almost certainly contains species of animals and plants which are still undiscovered. Why are scientists interested in finding out about new species of both plants and animals? **(Level 5)**

◀ Could 'Hobbits' still be living here?

Changing views

Scientists have always thought that intelligent animals have bigger brains. They have also thought that only intelligent animals make and use tools.

The evidence in the cave shows that the 'Hobbit' made and used tools. This means it must have been intelligent even though it had a small brain.

Scientists sometimes have to change their views when new scientific evidence becomes available that disproves a theory. But evidence can also be used to support a theory.

> **D** Explain why scientists were surprised to find tools with the 'Hobbit' skeleton. (Level 6)

▲ Intelligent animals can make and use tools

2.8 All alone

The Galapagos Islands in South America are home to many amazing animals and plants. One of them is Lonesome George who is thought to be the only surviving tortoise of his species. There used to be many more like George but goats were introduced to the island and ate the plants which the tortoises used for food. Sailors also hunted the tortoises for food.

George was rescued and taken to the Charles Darwin Research Station in the Galapagos Islands, where he still lives. Scientists have offered a $10,000 reward for a female tortoise of the same species as George.

- Write a list of other animals you know about that are in danger of becoming extinct.

- Lonesome George's habitat was damaged by the introduction of goats to Pinta Island in the Galapagos. Suggest what could be done to undo this damage so that the habitat could return to what it was like before.

- Do you think it is right to keep George in captivity?

Coming up in this Chapter ...

2.9 Home sweet home!

Learn about:
- how different environments have different features
- how living things are adapted to live in their habitat

The Arctic is one of the coldest ▶ environments on Earth

In 2002, a team of 50 scientists from the USA, Canada, China and Japan arrived in the Arctic aboard the ship *Louis St Laurent*. They were going to investigate the hidden life under the ice using remote-controlled vehicles.

The Arctic is a very important environment and scientists are studying it because they are worried that the temperature on Earth has started to rise.

A Why are scientists studying the Arctic? (Level 3)

Cold and windy

Different environments have different **environmental features,** such as different amounts of sunlight, amounts of water, soil conditions and temperatures. For example, a rainforest is hot and wet, while a desert is hot and dry.

The Inuit people are Arctic hunters ▼

In the Arctic, the ground is frozen solid for most of the year. The ocean is deep and mostly covered with frozen sea water or pack ice which drifts as the winds blow. During the Arctic winter it is dark for 24 hours each day, while during the summer it is always light. Most of the rain that falls in the Arctic falls as snow.

B Make a list of the features which make survival hard in the Arctic environment. (Level 4)

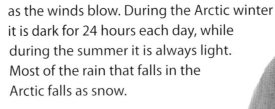

It is difficult for animals ▶ and plants to survive in the Arctic

48

Life in the frozen Arctic

A **habitat** is where an organism lives. The organisms which live in the habitat are adapted to survive there.

Animals such as polar bears, seals, lemmings and caribou live in the Arctic. Some animals have a thick layer of fat under their skins called blubber. Thick fur and blubber help to keep Arctic animals warm in the sub-zero temperatures. The scientists on the 2002 expedition had to wear specially designed clothing so that they could survive.

> **C** Seals have blubber and polar bears have thick fur. Why do humans have to wear specially designed clothing in the Arctic to survive? (Level 5)

▲ The thick layer of blubber under the skin insulates the seal from the cold

Other adaptations

Animals have other adaptations which help them to survive in the Arctic. Some animals, such as the Arctic fox, snowy owl and polar bear, have white coats which act as **camouflage** in the snow.

The harsh conditions in the Arctic mean that only grasses, mosses, lichen and some shrubs can grow there. There are no trees for animals to shelter under. Arctic plants are low growing with fuzzy coverings on the stem, leaves and buds. They also grow close together. These features help them to survive cold winds and blowing snow. The plants grow quickly for a short time during the Arctic summer.

◀ Equipped for survival

> **D** Why do Arctic plants only grow for a short period in the summer months? (Level 6)

> **Keywords**
> camouflage,
> environmental feature, habitat

49

2.10 What a difference a day makes

Learn about:
- how the conditions in a habitat can change over 24 hours
- how animals and plants are adapted to survive these changes

All change ▲
▶

Angus is a student at Leeds University. He is studying woodland near Leeds and he has set up a camera which takes photos every 15 minutes. His photos show that some animals share the woodland habitat. Some animals come out during the day and other animals come out during the night.

Scientists call animals that are awake during the day **diurnal**. Those that are awake at night are called **nocturnal**.

Equipped for seeing at night ▼

> **A** If nocturnal animals are awake at night, what do you think they do during the day? (Level 3)

Day and night

The environmental conditions in a habitat change over 24 hours. Animals and plants have to adapt to these changes if they are to survive. For example, in the woodland that Angus is studying, it is light during the day and dark at night.

Most nocturnal animals have large eyes with wide pupils to collect all the available light. This helps them to see at night. Their eyes may have special eyelids to protect them from bright daylight. They often have good senses of smell and hearing to help them hunt in the dark.

> **B** Why do nocturnal animals have large eyes with wide pupils? (Level 4)

Hot and cold

The temperature of some environments can change a lot over 24 hours. Deserts, for example, can be very hot during the day but very cold at night. These extremes can make survival difficult.

Some diurnal animals living in the desert protect themselves from the fierce heat by spending most of the day in any shade they can find. They make nests at night to help them survive the cold.

Rock pool

A rock pool is a very difficult environment to live in. Conditions can change a lot in 24 hours.

Feeling hot, hot, hot! ▲

We are studying rock pools on the beach to see how the organisms that live in them are adapted to survive.

The main change in conditions is that the tide comes in and goes out twice a day.

Bladderwrack

- Covered in gooey slime
- Stuck to the rock
- Rounded bumps contain air which helps the bladderwrack to float

Barnacle

- Cone-shaped shells
- Stuck to the rock
- Can close the opening at the top to trap water inside

When the tide is in, organisms are surrounded by water. When the tide is out, organisms are exposed to the air. This means they could dry out. The force of the tide going in and out could also carry organisms out to sea.

C Why are barnacles and bladderwrack stuck to the rocks? (Level 5)

D How are barnacles adapted to life when the tide is out? (Level 6)

Keywords
diurnal, nocturnal

Scientists at work

Scientists study rock pools to check for water pollution. They often find sewage, bacteria, oil and other chemicals in the water as well as litter left by visitors to the beach.

2.11 The changing seasons

Learn about:
- how habitats vary through the year
- how animals and plants survive seasonal changes

Winter and summer ▲ ▶

Squirrels often bury nuts in gardens ▼

Rachel is a keen gardener. During the summer, when the days are long and it is warm, she is busy outside cutting the grass and pulling up weeds. Plants grow well in summer.

During the winter, when it gets dark early, Rachel can't do much gardening. It is usually too cold and the ground can be frozen.

You can see that the same habitat can be very different during summer and winter. Animals and plants have to adapt and behave differently if they are to survive.

Food

Animals often eat more in summer when there is plenty of food. They build up layers of fat under their skin, ready for winter when there isn't so much food. Some animals bury food in case they need it later.

A How will burying nuts help squirrels survive in winter? (Level 3)

Going to sleep

Some animals **hibernate** so that they can survive winter. They go into a deep sleep so that they need much less energy to survive. The hedgehog in the photo on the next page has built up fat over the summer. Without the fat it would not survive hibernation.

Scientists don't yet fully understand what causes some animals to hibernate. Some scientists think it may be to do with hormones. This information could be useful to doctors in the future because they could put patients into hibernation during operations. This would mean that they would need less oxygen and there would be less risk of tissue damage. This is an example of how using science could change the way that doctors work.

B How does hibernation help an animal to survive? (Level 4)

C Some animals do not survive hibernation. What might be the reason for this? (Level 5)

Flying south

Some birds **migrate** to warmer climates in the winter. Swallows leave the UK to spend the winter in tropical Africa. Pink-footed geese leave Iceland to come here for a milder winter.

Plants in winter

The low light levels in winter in many habitats make it difficult for plants to make their food. Many plants lose their leaves during winter. Some plants survive as seeds which grow into new plants in the spring. Others, like bluebells, survive underground as bulbs. Scientists say that these plants become **dormant** during cold weather. This means that they are not active.

Sleeping away the winter ▲

Knowing what to do

Animals always seem to know what to do when the seasons change or when the time of day changes. Scientists who study the **behaviour** of animals are called **ethologists**, and this branch of science is called **ethology**. Ethologists carry out experiments in the laboratory as well as collecting data in the field.

Ethologists often study bird migration. They think that some birds migrate because they respond to days getting shorter in autumn, while other birds respond to harsh weather conditions.

Sooty shearwaters, a species of sea bird, can travel up to 40,000 miles around the Pacific Ocean when they migrate. In 2005, scientists in New Zealand fitted 33 shearwaters with electronic tags so they could track the birds' journeys. They collected data from 20 birds. The data showed that some birds travelled up to 910 km in a day.

▲ This tree has lost its leaves for the winter

D Scientists think that the temperature of the sea might be rising, which may affect when the different seasons happen. Suggest how this might affect sooty shearwater migration. (Level 6)

Scientists at work

In the USA, whooping cranes were taught new, safe migratory routes using a microlight, a type of motorised hang-glider, which they followed thinking it was a big bird.

Keywords
behaviour, dormant, ethologist, ethology, hibernate, migrate

2.12 Best behaviour!

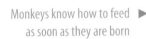

Monkeys know how to feed ▶ as soon as they are born

Newborn monkeys usually begin to feed immediately. They are born with the ability to suckle. Behaviours which animals have when they are born are called **innate** or **instinctive**. Cuckoos lay a single egg in other birds' nests. As soon as the baby cuckoo hatches, it pushes all the other eggs out of the nest so that the parent birds only have it to care for. Humans are also born with innate behaviours.

Baby monkeys eventually begin to feed themselves, but it takes a while for them to learn how to do this. Scientists call this a **learned behaviour**. Innate and learned behaviours work together to help animals survive.

Learned behaviours develop through experience as the animal gets older, so that it can live successfully in its environment. Humans have to learn skills such as talking and walking, and this can take several years.

Interesting fact

Newborn babies can grasp objects and can even swim underwater!

 Small children have to learn how to walk

A How does the innate behaviour of the cuckoo chick help it to survive? (Level 3)

Signal to act

Humans, like other animals, respond to **signals** or **stimuli** which trigger different kinds of behaviour. Signals can be internal or external. A tiny baby will cry if it is hungry or if its nappy needs changing. Being hungry or uncomfortable are internal signals. It will also cry if it is startled by something nearby. A loud noise might be an external signal.

Birds are born knowing how to build a particular shape and size of nest at the right time of year. Scientists think that birds respond to external signals in the environment, such as the amount of daylight and temperature level.

Signals in the environment tell ▶ birds when to build their nest

B Why might different birds living in different environments need different types of nest? (Level 4)

Lorenz was the first thing these geese saw when they hatched ▲

Studying behaviour

Konrad Lorenz was a famous Austrian biologist who was interested in how animals behave. He showed that young geese are born with an innate behaviour to follow the first object they see when they hatch, because they think it will care for them. Usually this is their mother, but Lorenz showed that geese will follow other things too.

Finches inside the choice chamber ▼

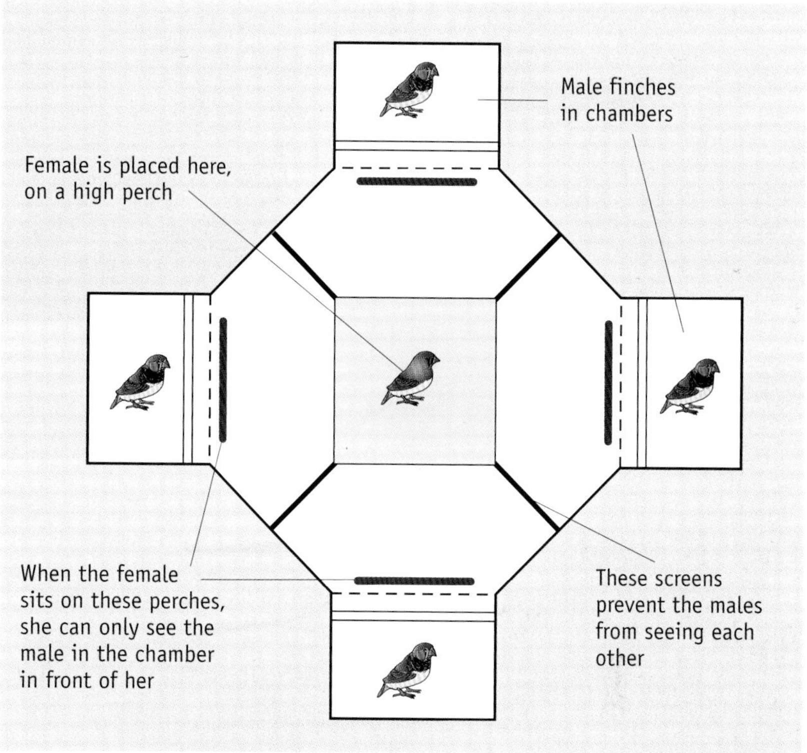

Male finches in chambers

Female is placed here, on a high perch

When the female sits on these perches, she can only see the male in the chamber in front of her

These screens prevent the males from seeing each other

Choosing a mate

Male zebra finches have coloured bands on their legs. Sanjay designs an experiment to see if a female Zebra finch chooses a male because of the colour of his leg bands. The experiment includes a special cage called a choice chamber, in which:

- a female finch can see four different males
- she is able to perch in front of each one
- as she moves from perch to perch, the time spent looking at each male is recorded.

Sanjay predicts that the more interested the female is in a male, the more time she will spend looking at him. He does this experiment with different combinations of 10 males and 10 females. The bar graph shows his results.

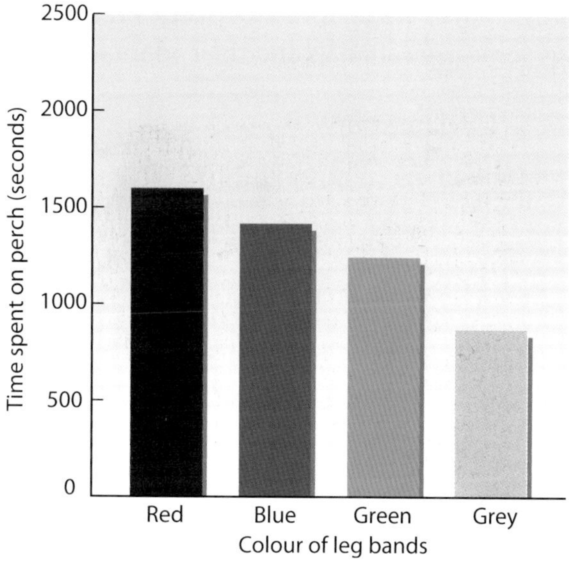

C Sanjay uses a large sample of finches in this investigation. Why is it important to use a large sample? (Level 5)

D Sanjay studies zebra finches 'in captivity'. You can also study animals 'in the wild'. What are the advantages and disadvantages of each method of observing animals? (Level 6)

Keywords
innate behaviour, instinctive behaviour, learned behaviour, signals, stimuli

[Bar graph: y-axis "Time spent on perch (seconds)" from 0 to 2500; x-axis "Colour of leg bands" with bars: Red ≈1600, Blue ≈1400, Green ≈1200, Grey ≈850]

2.13 Fit for purpose?

Adapted to capture, kill and eat its prey ▲

A tiger stalks through the forest in India, hunting for its next meal. Tigers are **predators**. Scientists say that tigers have **adaptations**. This means that they have special features that make them good at being predators. For example, tigers' teeth are adapted for killing and eating their **prey**.

Tigers are strong and can use their strength to knock their prey off balance. A single blow from a tiger's paw could kill you. Tigers can reach up to 60 km/h when they are running and can jump up to 5 m. They are also good swimmers and can kill prey in the water.

A Make a list of the features that help to make a tiger a good predator. (Level 3)

Adapted as prey

Simon is doing research on how prey animals are adapted to escape predators. He has created a table which shows some prey animals and their adaptations.

Prey animal	Adaptation
porcupine	shoots out its spines
skunk	produces a bad smell
squid	shoots out a cloud of 'ink'
deer	can run and leap very fast
zebra	stripes act as camouflage

▲ Porcupines can release their spines when threatened by a predator

B How do you think a porcupine's spines help protect it from a predator? (Level 4)

C A rabbit frightened by a predator runs away. It has a white undertail. How does this adaptation help other rabbits to escape? (Level 5)

Producers and consumers

Animals are **consumers**. They get their energy from eating plants or other animals. Plants are **producers**. They use light energy to make their food. Leaves are adapted for this job. They are usually green and broad. The green colour comes from a pigment in the leaves called chlorophyll. Chlorophyll traps light energy. Broad leaves can catch a lot of light.

▲ This leaf is adapted as a light collector

▲ This poisonous frog is a consumer. It is also preyed on and its colours warn predators to keep away

A successful ▶ herbivore

Consumers can be **herbivores**, **carnivores** or **omnivores**. Herbivores eat only plants and carnivores eat only animals. Omnivores eat both plants and animals. Humans are omnivores, although some people think it is wrong to eat animals for ethical or religious reasons.

D James went for a walk in his garden and saw fox tracks in some soft earth, rabbit droppings on the grass, a blackbird in a tree, blackberries in a hedge, owl pellets on the shed floor and a woodlouse under some pots. Make a list of the producers and consumers James has observed. (Level 6)

Foul fact

Rabbits eat their droppings. They digest their food twice in order to get enough energy from the plants they eat.

Keywords
adaptation, carnivore, consumer, herbivore, omnivore, predator, prey, producer

2.14 Who eats what?

Learn about:
- what food chains are
- how food chains are linked together

Shark attack ▲

Australian diver caught in the jaws of a great white

Eric Nerhus was caught in the mouth and jaws of a great white shark, the most fearsome predator in the sea. His head, a shoulder and an arm were fully inside the shark's mouth and 3,000 teeth were biting down on his body.

'It started to shake me,' said the 41-year-old diver. 'I thought, "Oh no, that is when they cut the biggest piece of meat off you." I poked my fingers into the eye socket and when it opened its mouth a bit I wriggled out.'

The Florida Museum of Natural History keeps a worldwide shark attack file. There are now fewer attacks than there used to be. Scientists suggest this may be due to falling numbers of sharks, as well as swimmers being more cautious about shark attacks.

Food chains

Great white sharks don't usually eat humans. They usually feed on fish, seals and turtles, which in turn eat smaller fish, shrimps and crabs. These consume tiny plants in the seawater called **phytoplankton**.

Scientists use the idea of **food chains** to show the **feeding relationships** between animals and plants. Plants as producers are always at the bottom of food chains. They are the only living things that can produce food using light **energy** trapped by their leaves.

| plankton | shrimp | seal | shark |

▲ An ocean food chain

A What is the producer in the ocean food chain? (Level 3)

Food webs

Most consumers feed on a variety of living things. Scientists link food chains together into **food webs**. The diagram shows an ocean food web.

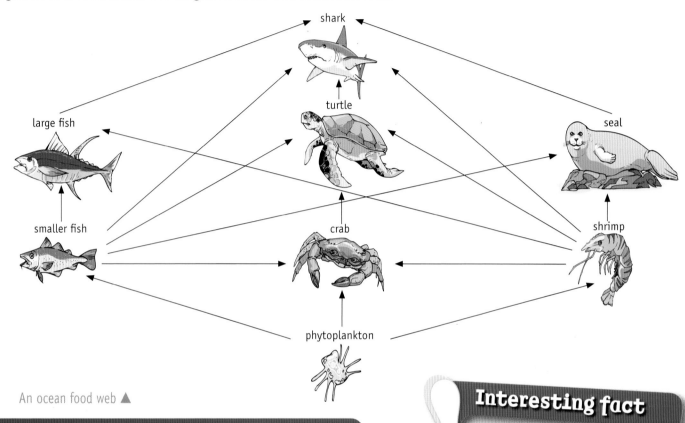

An ocean food web ▲

B Find as many food chains as you can within the ocean food web. (Level 4)

Interdependence

Great white sharks catch large fish, which eat small fish, which feed on phytoplankton. The number of small fish depends on the amount of phytoplankton available for them to eat. It also depends on the number of large fish and on the number of great white sharks that eat the large fish. In this way, living things depend on each other – they are **interdependent**.

Look at the ocean food web.

C What would happen to the number of large fish if the number of sharks increased? (Level 5)

D What would happen if all the shrimps died? (Level 6)

Interesting fact

Great white sharks can detect one drop of blood in 100 litres of sea water. They hunt by following the electricity that every animal produces.

Keywords
energy, feeding relationship, food chain, food web, interdependent, phytoplankton

Learn about:
- how barn owls are threatened by loss of their habitat
- how animals can be protected by protecting their habitat

Barn owl populations are under threat ▲

I don't want to disturb the owls, but I'd like to repair these buildings. People need homes and these barns would provide some. I'd use the money from selling the barns to plant more hedges, to provide habitats for the animals that the owls eat. Lots of hedges have been cut down in this area, so there's less food for the owls.

Mr Jones is a farmer. He has some very old and derelict farm buildings. They are no longer used for storing machinery and are falling down. But there is a pair of barn owls nesting in them. Barn owls like to use the same nesting place year after year.

Interesting old buildings must be kept for future generations to see. If the barns are made into homes, they will be preserved instead of falling down. But there are barn owls in the buildings. I've seen owl pellets on the ground containing the remains of the small animals the owls eat. We need a barn owl expert to advise us.

Barn owls prefer to live in buildings such as old barns and they use the same nesting place year after year. It's possible to turn barns into homes if we provide places or nest boxes for the owls to nest. I can survey a site and help planners, builders and architects design buildings where both people and owls can live.

Planning officer Adam is concerned about the farm buildings because they are very old and of historical interest. He would allow them to be restored – but the barn owls must be protected. The Barn Owl Trust can help.

Tracey works for the Barn Owl Trust as a conservation officer. The Trust advises farmers and erects nest boxes. They know a lot about what barn owls eat, how they live and their habitats. They give advice about barn owls and work closely with planning officers and developers to protect nesting sites.

A Why is it important for the Barn Owl Trust to know a lot about how barn owls live? (Level 3)

B How does an unploughed strip around a field help the animals and plants survive in the habitat? (Level 4)

Foul fact

Owls cannot digest the bones, fur and feathers of their prey, so they cough these up in 'pellets'.

Owl pellets show exactly what an owl has eaten ▼

Scientists at work

Scientists can study where owls go by tagging them. The owls wear little backpacks and harnesses. CCTV is also used to follow the survival of young birds.

C Why is it important to provide owls with a nest box very close to their original home? (Level 5)

D How would the contents of owl pellets help scientists to understand the feeding requirements of barn owls, so that they could release them into suitable areas? (Level 6)

2 Assess your progress

2.2 The same but different

1 Copy and complete the sentences below using these words:

species   fertile   features

Scientists say that living things which have the most _____ in common belong to the same _____ . Its members can breed together to produce _____ offspring. (Level 3)

2 David reads in the newspaper that the local zoo has had a new arrival. The new baby is a liger. Which animals have bred together to produce this animal? (Level 3)

3 Michael noticed that his hair and eye colour are the same as his grandfather's. Explain how this could happen. (Level 4)

4 Jasmine's dog is a labradoodle. Its mother is a poodle and its father is a labrador. The labradoodle has just had a litter of pups. Explain why it is possible for a labrador and a poodle to breed and produce fertile offspring. (Level 5)

5 Jasmine's labradoodle has curly fur like a poodle but mostly looks like a labrador. Using the keywords **feature** and **inherited**, explain why it looks like this. (Level 6)

2.3 Sort it out!

1 Scientists have tried to work out how many organisms exist on Earth. What is the most likely estimate of this? (Level 3)

2 The largest groups of living things which scientists use in classification are kingdoms. What are the main two kingdoms called? (Level 3)

3 Why do scientists all over the world use the same Latin names for organisms? (Level 4)

4 Look at the photo of the insect on page 36. Make a list of features that you would look at if you were the scientist who found it, and wanted to name and classify it. (Level 5)

5 **a** What might scientists use in the future to help them classify living things? **b** Predict what scientists might notice if they compared the genes of a gorilla, a chimpanzee and a human. (Level 6)

2.4 Spineless!

1 Explain what invertebrates are. (Level 3)

2 Why are invertebrates important to baleen whales? (Level 3)

2 What makes bumblebees the 'gardener's friend'? (Level 4)

3 What can gardeners do to improve the habitat for bumblebees? (Level 5)

4 Ladybirds and aphids are both invertebrates. Aphids feed on rose bushes and damage them. Rose growers sometimes release ladybirds onto their roses to eat the aphids. Explain why this is better than using chemicals to control the aphids. (Level 6)

2.5 The bare bones about vertebrates

1 Where do amphibians lay their eggs? (Level 3)

2 **a** Which vertebrate group produces eggs with a leathery shell?
b List two other features of organisms from this vertebrate group. (Level 3)

3 Birds and mammals are two vertebrate groups which care for their young. Why do they do this? (Level 4)

4 The golden poison dart frog produces a deadly poison. Not all frogs have this characteristic but all frogs belong to the same vertebrate group.
a What is this group called? **b** List the features which members of this group share. (Level 5)

5 The duck-billed platypus and echidna are unusual mammals. Compare and contrast their features with those of other mammals. (Level 6)

2.6 Putting plants in their place

1 What features do all the plants on page 43 have in common? (Level 3)

2 Which group of plants does the 'corpse plant' belong to? (Level 3)

3 How are plants that make seeds classified? (Level 4)

4 Why does the corpse plant smell of decaying flesh when it flowers? (Level 5)

5 Kew Gardens contains a collection of plants from all over the world and is a valuable scientific resource. Explain the ways in which the collection of plants at Kew helps scientists to study and protect plants. (Level 6)

2.7 Investigating the unknown

1 What event caused many of the living things on Flores island to die out 12,000 years ago? (Level 3)

2 Why do scientists consult museums when they make new discoveries? (Level 4)

3 Scientists can easily take samples of genetic material from living human beings. They might be able to get a sample from the 'Hobbit' remains. How might these samples of genetic material be of use in identifying species which are closely related to the 'Hobbit'? (Level 5)

4 The 'Hobbit' was found with a collection of tools. Only more intelligent animals use tools. What types of tool might have been found with the 'Hobbit' and what might they have been used for? (Level 6)

2.9 Home sweet home!

1 Copy and complete the sentences using the words below:

**habitat   light   temperature
availability of water   adapted**

A place where an organism lives is called its _____. These have different environmental features such as _____, _____ and _____. Organisms which live in a habitat are said to be _____ to live there. (Level 3)

2 How is an Arctic fox adapted to survive in the Arctic environment? (Level 3)

3 How are animals such as seals and whales able to survive in the Arctic? (Level 4)

4 Arctic plants grow close to the frozen ground crowded together in groups. Explain how this helps them survive the cold winds and low temperatures. (Level 5)

5 Why is finding water to drink a problem for animals in the Arctic? (Level 6)

Chapter 2 questions continued on next page

2 Assess your progress

2.10 What a difference a day makes

1 What is the main difference between nocturnal and diurnal animals? (Level 3)

2 What is the main change that occurs in a rock pool every day? (Level 3)

3 How do temperature and light levels in a desert environment change over 24 hours? (Level 4)

4 Bladderwrack is a plant. It needs light to produce food energy. How is it adapted to position itself in the light when the tide is in? (Level 5)

5 Conditions in woodland habitats change a great deal over 24 hours. You can use a light meter and a temperature sensor to monitor how these change. Predict how the temperature and level of light will change from midnight to midday in winter. (Level 6)

2.11 The changing seasons

1 Why do animals that hibernate need to eat a lot as winter approaches? (Level 3)

2 Some birds leave Britain for the winter, while others arrive here from other countries. Why do birds migrate like this? (Level 3)

3 Why do scientists investigate hibernation? (Level 4)

4 Omar has had his kitten for a year. 'My cat loses a lot of hair when the better weather comes in spring,' he says. 'In winter she grows a really thick coat.' Explain his observation. (Level 5)

5 Plants are affected by seasonal changes, particularly changes in the light level. **a** Explain why the light level is important to plants. **b** Describe how the growth of plants differs in summer and winter. (Level 6)

2.12 Best behaviour!

1 You saw on page 55 that Konrad Lorenz noticed that young geese become attached to objects or animals that they see soon after birth. How did he show this to other scientists? (Level 3)

2 Sophie's cat has had a litter of kittens. The mother cat is still feeding the kittens, but soon Sophie will start to give them special kitten food to eat. The kittens do not have to learn to feed from their mother. What kind of behaviour is this? (Level 3)

3 Read about Sanjay's experiment with the Zebra finches on page 55 and answer the following questions: **a** Which leg colour was most attractive to the female finches? **b** Which was least attractive? (Level 4)

4 Kittens spend quite a lot of time playing and fighting with the rest of the litter. This helps them develop hunting skills. **a** What are the factors that turn a kitten into a good hunter? **b** How do innate and learned behaviours work together to help a kitten survive? (Level 5)

5 In Sanjay's choice chamber, the male birds could not see each other. Why did Sanjay design this into the investigation? (Level 6)

6 When Sanjay carried out his investigation into finch behaviour, he was careful to make sure there was no outside noise, no draughts, no change in temperature or light level. **a** Why was this good experimental design? **b** How might these factors affect the finches? (Level 6)

2.13 Fit for purpose?

1 Fill in the missing words in the sentences using the words below:

prey   predators   consumers   producers

Plants are _____ and animals are _____. Animals that eat other animals are called _____. The animals that they eat are called _____.
(Level 3)

2 Explain the difference between carnivores, herbivores and omnivores. (Level 3)

3 Gazelles are prey animals and they often have long, sharp horns. How does this help them to survive? (Level 4)

4 The canopy (top layer) of the rainforest is dense and does not let much light through. There are climbing plants in the forest that grow around tree trunks to climb up to the top. Why do they do this? (Level 5)

5 Lions hunt zebras but their attacks are not always successful. How do the following help the zebra to survive? **a** a striped coat; **b** the ability to kick out with its hind legs; **c** agility when running. (Level 6)

2.14 Who eats what?

1 What do food chains show? (Level 3)

2 Put the words fox and rabbit in the spaces below to complete this food chain:
lettuce → _____ → _____ (Level 3)

3 Put the organisms in this list into a food chain: cow, human, grass. (Level 4)

4 Rabbits and sheep eat grass. Add these consumers to the food chain you have drawn for question 3. Remember that humans eat all of these animals. You are now building a food web. (Level 5)

5 Rabbits are primary consumers because they eat plants. Foxes, which eat rabbits, are called secondary consumers. What are the primary and secondary consumers in this list: hares, field mice, sparrow hawks and kestrels? (Level 6)

2.15 Conversation in action

1 Make a list of animals that barn owls might eat. Think about small mammals and amphibians. (Level 3)

2 Why are hedges an important part of the owl's habitat? (Level 4)

3 **a** Why do barn owls need lots of small mammals living around them? **b** Why do barn owls have to hunt over a large area? (Level 5)

4 Think carefully about what the farmer, the planning officer and the conservation worker told you on pages 60 and 61. They each have a point of view. Imagine that you are the chief planning officer for the area who will decide what is to be done with the barns. Write down a question you would like to ask each person to help you make a decision. (Level 6)

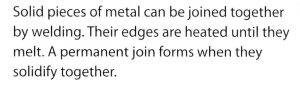

3.1 A world of tiny particles

Solid pieces of metal can be joined together by welding. Their edges are heated until they melt. A permanent join forms when they solidify together.

Welding even works underwater. The diver can breathe underwater because air can be squashed or compressed into a small cylinder. He can swim through the water because it flows around him. All of these things and more can be explained using the idea of tiny particles that we cannot even see.

- Substances can be solid, liquid or gas. For example, water is a liquid. Write down at least two examples each of a solid, a liquid and a gas.

- What happens to the edges of the metal when the welder heats them?

- How would you separate a mixture of sand and water? Draw the equipment you would use.

Coming up in this Chapter ...

3.2 A gritty problem

Learn about:
- some differences between sand and salt
- how to get table salt from rock salt

These mountains of salt come from seawater ▲

Too much salt in your diet can lead to high blood pressure. But your body needs salt to stay healthy. It helps your muscles and nerves work properly.

The sea is salty and you can get salt from it. You can also get salt from **rock salt**. This is a mixture of rough sand and salt that is mined from deep underground. Most of the salt in the UK comes from rock salt. So why are there no bits of sand in your salt?

Table salt from rock salt

Salt is **soluble**. It dissolves in water. The salt and water mix completely to make a clear salt **solution**. Sand is **insoluble**. It does not dissolve in water. Instead, tiny bits of sand make the water cloudy and bigger bits sink to the bottom.

A What is the difference between a substance that is soluble in water and a substance that is insoluble in water? (Level 3)

You wouldn't like to eat rock salt. Its sand would wear away your teeth. So the sand has to be separated from the salt. You could do this using your fingers, but it would take a long time! There is an easier way:

- add water to the rock salt
- stir to dissolve the salt
- filter the mixture of sand, salt and water.

Look at the photo on the next page. Sand does not dissolve, so it stays behind on the filter paper. It is called the **residue**. The liquid that drips through the filter paper is clear and colourless. It is called the **filtrate**. It looks just like water, but is actually salt solution.

▲ Rock salt

Table salt ▶

The final step

You cannot filter salt solution to get solid bits of salt back. The salt is dissolved in water and just goes through the filter paper. You have to **evaporate** the water from the salt solution. You warm up the salt solution to evaporate most of the water, before leaving the dish for a few days. Crystals of table salt form in the dish as the water evaporates.

▲ Salt solution drips through filter paper but the sand does not

C How can you tell that salt solution contains salt, without tasting it? (Level 5)

D Describe how salt can be obtained from a salt pan in a hot country. (Level 6)

◄ Water can be removed from the salt solution by evaporation

◄ Salt appears when water evaporates from salt solution

Keywords
evaporate, filtrate, insoluble, residue, rock salt, soluble, solution

3.3 What's the solution?

Swimmers in the Blue Lagoon at Svartsengi in Iceland ▲

Hot waste water from a nearby geothermal power plant fills the Blue Lagoon. It contains silica and other dissolved minerals. These also make a rich mud. Bathers discovered in the 1980s that the water and mud help skin problems, such as eczema. People from all over the world now come to bathe here.

The total mass stays the same when a solute dissolves in a solvent ▼

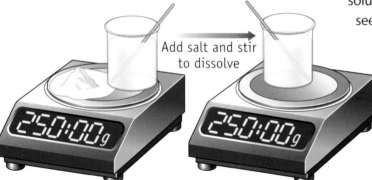

Add salt and stir to dissolve

When a solid dissolves in water, you see bits mixing with the water. Later, all the bits seem to have disappeared. You have made a clear solution. The Blue Lagoon water helps skin get better. So it seems likely that the dissolved solids are still there, even though we cannot see them. But is this true?

Does it disappear?

It is easy to find out if a dissolved solid is still there. You weigh the solid and the water before dissolving, and then again after dissolving. The mass stays the same. So the solid must still be there, even if you cannot see it. A scientist would say that the mass is **conserved**.

A What happens to the total mass when a solid dissolves in water? (Level 3)

B 2 g of salt is dissolved in 50 g of water. What is the mass of the salt solution? (Level 4)

Salt flats form when all the water ▶ evaporates from a lake or sea

Concentrated solutions

The solid that dissolves is the **solute**. The liquid that dissolves it is the **solvent**. A solution becomes more **concentrated** if you keep dissolving more solute. But there is a limit to how much solute will dissolve. When no more will dissolve, the solution is a **saturated** solution.

For example, some people like sugar in their tea. The more sugar they stir in, the more concentrated it becomes. The more concentrated it is, the sweeter the tea tastes. When no more sugar will dissolve, the tea is saturated with sugar. It would taste very sweet indeed.

▲ A cup of sweet tea contains dissolved sugar

> **C** What is the solvent in a cup of sweet tea? Name one solute it contains. (Level 4)

Speeding up dissolving

There are several ways you can speed up dissolving. Stirring helps a solute dissolve faster. Small bits dissolve faster than big lumps. And powders dissolve really quickly. Solutes dissolve faster when the solvent is hot. Sugar dissolves faster in hot tea than it does in cold tea. But then most people don't like cold tea anyway.

> **D** Suggest why hot water is used to wash dirty dishes instead of cold water. (Level 5)

Interesting fact

The solvents used in car paints evaporate easily and can make harmful fumes. Paint sprayers wear protective clothing and masks to keep them safe.

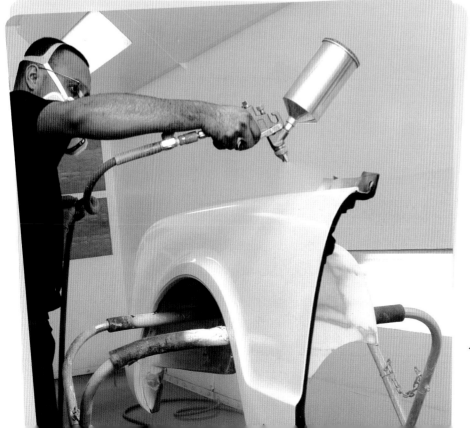

Keywords
concentrated, conserved, saturated, solute, solvent

◀ Water is not the only solvent. Car paint contains a mixture of solvents

3.4 Go with the flow

Learn about:
- the tiny particles that everything is made from
- how these particles behave in solids, liquids and gases
- why liquids and gases can flow freely

Scientists need to know about ▶ liquids to build complex pumps

Interesting fact

Particles vibrate and move all the time. They would only stop at a chilly −273.15 °C. But nothing can get this cold.

Scientists and engineers need to know why **solids**, **liquids** and **gases** have different properties and behave in different ways. It helps them design chemicals and machines for particular jobs. Solids, liquids and gases are the three **states of matter**.

The tiny bits that everything is made from are too small to see. So a scientific **model** is needed. This helps scientists imagine what these tiny bits do in solids, liquid and gases.

> **A** Why do scientists and engineers need to know about the different properties of solids, liquids and gases? (Level 3)

The particle theory

All the substances around you have something in common with a sandcastle. They are made of tiny **particles**, just as sand is made of grains. But these particles are so tiny we cannot see them.

For example, each sand grain is made from over ten billion billion particles of a substance called silica. Forces attract particles to each other and stick them together, just as water can stick sand grains together in a sandcastle.

The particles are arranged and move differently in each state of matter.

Damp sand lets you make great sandcastles ▲

The states of matter

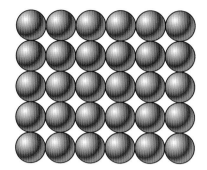
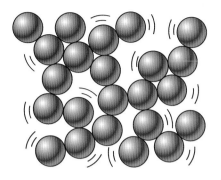
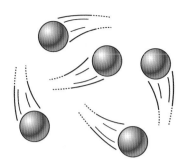

The particles in solids are packed closely together in an ordered way. The particles can only vibrate, and forces between them stop them moving from place to place.

The particles in liquids are packed closely together, but they are jumbled up in a random way. There are fewer forces between them so the particles can move around each other.

The particles in gases are far apart and are randomly arranged. There are almost no forces between them and they constantly move in all directions.

B In which two states are (i) the particles packed closely together? (ii) the particles randomly arranged? (Level 4)

Flowing liquids and gases

The forces between particles in solids stop the particles moving from place to place. If you drop an ice cube into an empty glass, it cannot flow to fill the bottom. But liquids and gases can flow.

C Why does solid rock not flow? (Level 5)

If you pour a drink into the glass, the liquid fills the bottom. This is because the particles in liquids can move over each other.

The particles in gases move in all directions. So gases flow to completely fill their container, whatever its size and shape.

D The runnier a liquid is, the weaker the forces between its particles. Explain which liquid: lemon juice or syrup has the strongest forces between its particles. (Level 6)

▲ Solid rock cannot flow but hot liquid rock can

Keywords
gas, liquid, model, particle, solid, state of matter

3.5 ALIEN SCIENCE TEACHER

Learn about

- investigating a problem and analysing the results
- how to separate coloured substances

Newsflash

Are there aliens in our schools?
Scientists have detected some strange electrical activity at a local school. They suspect that one or more of the science teachers are aliens from a distant planet. The highest levels of activity are detected at the same time every week when the Young Engineers Club is being held.

A spokesperson for the scientists told reporters today, 'We have narrowed it down to three suspects, Mr Albert, Miss Benton and Mrs Chandler because they run the Club at that time.'

Who is the alien? ▲

A Why do scientists think that one or more of the teachers might be an alien? (Level 3)

Before you start

The race is on to expose the aliens. You will need to organise yourselves into groups of four. There are three samples of blood to test and one person will need to jot down the results. If one of the teachers is an alien, their '*BLOOD*' will look normal but will have a blue substance in it!

What you will need

A sample of 'blood' has been provided by each of our suspect science teachers. You are going to use a method called **chromatography** and each group will need:

- samples of 'blood' from each of the teachers
- three pieces of filter paper
- beakers
- sterile pipettes (to avoid contamination).

> Chromatography is one of those scientific words that come from the Greek language. 'chroma' means 'colour' and 'graph' means 'write'.

What to do

1

Put the filter paper on top of a beaker.

2
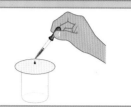
Take some of the 'blood' out of the vial with the pipette – don't spill any!

3
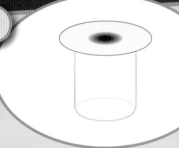
Carefully put one drop of 'blood' in the centre of the filter paper.

4
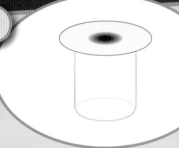
Let it spread out.

5

Add 5 drops of water, one drop at a time to the 'blood'. You should then see the colours separating on the paper.

> On wet paper, different coloured substances travel at different speeds, so they separate out. The colours that are not very soluble in water will not move as fast.

B The blue substance in alien blood is more soluble in water than the red substance. Which substance will travel further on the filter paper? (Level 4)

C Think about the coloured particles and the water particles. Draw or write down what you think might be happening in this experiment. (Level 5)

> Was it real blood?

Taking it further

The blood tests suggest that just one of the suspect teachers is an alien, but the scientists would like more evidence. Human saliva is weakly alkaline, but the scientists think that alien saliva will be strongly alkaline and would like you to do further tests.

> No! But it looked real and I've always thought that teacher was weird!

D How will you test the saliva samples? (Level 6)

Voted a Best Lesson at Selly Park Technology College for Girls

Keyword
chromatography

3.6 Mind the gap

Learn about:
- what particles do when substances dissolve
- why filtering works

Cornflakes can be used as a scientific model ▲

▲ Copper sulfate dissolves in water to make a clear blue solution

A notice on the side of packets of cornflakes often warns you that the contents may settle during transport. This is why the bag inside the box isn't full of cornflakes, even though it was filled to the top at the factory.

You haven't lost any cornflakes. Instead, the movement of the lorry has shaken them until they fit closely together. Most of the big gaps between the cornflakes have gone. This is one model for what happens to particles when substances mix together or dissolve.

Dissolving

When a solid solute dissolves in a solvent, its particles become evenly spread through the solvent. For example, copper sulfate is a blue solid. It dissolves in water to make blue copper sulfate solution. The diagram shows how this happens.

A **Which particles are free to move around: water particles or particles in a piece of copper sulfate? (Level 3)**

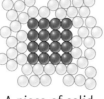

A piece of solid copper sulfate is added to water.

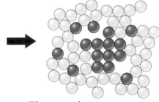

The moving water particles collide with the particles of copper sulfate. Each copper sulfate particle becomes surrounded by water particles.

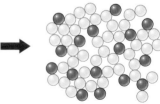

Copper sulfate particles are moved away from the rest of the copper sulfate until they become evenly mixed with water particles.

Filtering

You can separate an insoluble substance from a solution by filtering. For example, sand can be separated from salt solution by filtering. It works because filter paper has tiny holes in it. Pieces of sand are too big to go through these holes. But the salt particles in the salt solution are separated from each other by the water particles. This makes them small enough to go through the tiny holes.

B Explain how you know that water particles must be smaller than pieces of sand. (Level 4)

Where does it go?

Concrete is a very tough mixture. A typical recipe for concrete needs $0.25\,m^3$ of cement, $0.65\,m^3$ of sand and $0.90\,m^3$ of gravel. After mixing it all with water and letting it set, you get only $1\,m^3$ of concrete.

There are different possible explanations:

- The particles of cement, sand and gravel might shrink as the concrete sets.
- The pieces of gravel might have tiny holes between them that the cement and sand fall into.

A broken piece of concrete contains normal sized pieces of gravel surrounded by a grey mixture of sand and cement. So these explanations are not correct.

The particle theory can correctly explain the difference in volume. It says that the grains of cement and sand fill many of the gaps between the pieces of gravel. The same thing can happen when you dissolve one chemical in another.

C If you mix $50\,cm^3$ of ethanol with $50\,cm^3$ of water, you get only about $96\,cm^3$. Ruth added $5\,cm^3$ of ethanol to $5\,cm^3$ of water. Explain why it might be difficult to show that the total volume is less than $10\,cm^3$. (Level 5)

D Explain why the volume of a mixture of ethanol and water is less than the volume of its separate ingredients. (Level 6)

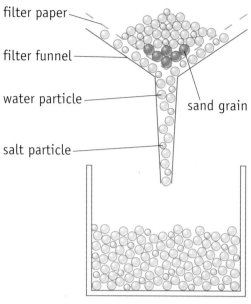

filter paper
filter funnel
water particle
sand grain
salt particle

▲ Dissolved particles are small enough to go through the filter paper

Interesting fact

Enough concrete is made in the world to give everyone a 1 tonne ball of it every birthday.

Keyword
concrete

▲ Concrete is used to make buildings, bridges and roads

3.7 Building bridges

Learn about:
- why some solids are difficult to stretch
- why solids and liquids are less easily squashed than gases

The Millau Viaduct in France was opened in 2004 ▲

The Millau Viaduct crosses the Tarn valley in southern France. It is made from over a quarter of a million tonnes of concrete and **steel**. The viaduct is the tallest road bridge in the world. The road deck weighs over 35,000 tonnes and hangs from steel cables attached to the towers.

Bridges and the materials they are made from have changed a lot over the centuries. They used to be made of wood and stone.

The engineers who designed and built this viaduct tested and chose the materials very carefully for their ability to carry heavy loads. They had to make sure that the viaduct would be safe to use.

Concrete and steel

The particles in solids are close together. They cannot be pushed any closer together. This makes it difficult to squash solids, so they keep their shape and volume.

Concrete is very good at resisting being squashed. But it is not so good at resisting being stretched. Steel resists being stretched much better than concrete. Strong forces join the particles in steel together and stop the metal being stretched easily.

▲ Concrete is widely used as a building material

> **A** Why is it difficult to squash concrete? (Level 3)

> **B** Why are steel cables used to hold the road deck instead of concrete? (Level 4)

The towers of the Millau Viaduct are made from steel-reinforced concrete. Each one is built from a cage of steel cables with concrete poured around them. The concrete resists being squashed and the steel resists being stretched. So the new 'composite material' resists squashing *and* stretching.

C Suggest why traditional plaster for walls may contain horse hair. (Level 5)

Brakes and tyres

Liquids are difficult to squash because the particles in liquids are close together. The particles cannot be pushed any closer together. Liquids change shape but they keep the same volume.

This is useful for car brakes. When the driver presses the brake pedal, the force acts through liquid in the brake pipes and is applied to the brakes. Using liquids like this is called hydraulics. Before hydraulic brakes were invented in 1918, cars used cable brakes just like bikes do today.

When you squash a gas, its particles move into the spaces between them. Gases change their shape and volume to fill their container. So a gas would be a poor choice for making bridges or filling brake pipes.

▲ Liquids are used in the hydraulic legs that move this aircraft flight simulator

But a gas is just right for filling tyres. As a tyre rolls over bumps, the air inside squashes and changes shape. This makes the ride more comfortable.

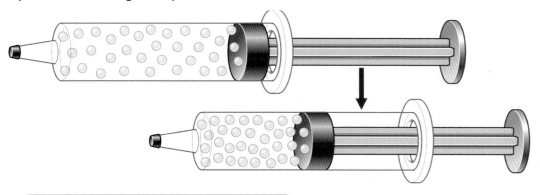

Keyword
steel

◄ Particles in a gas have space to move into

D Explain what would happen if air got into the brake pipes of a car. (Level 6)

Interesting fact

Reinforced concrete was invented in 1849 by a French gardener called Joseph Monier. He used it to make tough plant pots and tubs. But it was quickly used to make longer bridges than were possible before.

It is easy to squash ▶ balloons filled with air and change their shape

3.8 Stinky stinks

Learn about:
- liquids and gases spreading and mixing without being stirred

This pub in Norfolk was destroyed by a gas explosion ▲

Natural gas is used for cooking and heating, but gas leaks can cause explosions. So it is important that you can tell if gas is leaking. Ethanethiol (ee-thayn-thy-ol) smells a bit like rotten eggs. It is deliberately added to the gas. This way you can smell leaking gas, even in a different part of the house.

A bottle of perfume is opened in the room. After a while you can smell the perfume everywhere in the room. You drop a sugar lump into a cup of tea. It dissolves and after a while all the tea is sweet, even though you did not stir it. Just why do the ethanethiol, perfume and sugar spread without being stirred? The reason is a process called **diffusion**.

Diffusion spreads the smell of cooking through the air ▼

| A | **What makes natural gas smell? (Level 3)** |

Diffusion in gases

When you open a bottle of perfume, particles of perfume escape. But they don't just zoom out and straight into your nose. Instead, they bump into air particles on the way. This means it takes some time for the smell to reach you. Someone close to the bottle will smell the perfume before someone further away. The same thing happens with the smelly particles added to natural gas.

Gas particles mix evenly because of diffusion ▲

| B | **Why does the smell of a new air freshener take time to fill a room? (Level 4)** |

Diffusion in liquids

Diffusion happens more slowly in liquids than it does in gases. This is because the particles in liquids move more slowly. They can carry dissolved substances, like sugar, through all the liquid but it takes a long time. So people usually stir tea to completely mix their sugar.

C   Why is diffusion slower in liquids than it is in gases? (Level 5)

Speeding up diffusion

Diffusion happens faster at higher temperatures. This is because the particles move more quickly when they are heated. Evan carried out an experiment to see the effect of changing the temperature on the time taken for a smell to travel a short distance. The table shows his results.

Temperature against time

Temperature (°C)	Time (s)
20	302
40	292
60	283
80	275

D   Look at the results in the table. (i) Estimate the time taken for the smell to travel at 0 °C. (ii) Explain your answer. (iii) Suggest why you should repeat the experiment. (Level 6)

Can diffusion happen in solids?

I don't think so. The particles in a solid only vibrate and don't move around.

Why can you tell where a smell is coming from?

I think it's because particles move from where they are very concentrated to where they are not very concentrated.

Keyword
diffusion

▲ Particles from a purple crystal take several hours or even days to diffuse through water

Scientists at work

Engineers test gas pipes to see if they are gas tight. They use an electronic 'nose' to sniff for the gas outside the pipes.

3.9 Growing in the heat

Learn about:
- how and why substances change volume when their temperature changes

Many tropical islands are only just above sea level ▲

Global warming is causing the average temperature of the oceans to increase. As the seawater gets hotter, it **expands**. It takes up more room, causing the sea level to slowly increase.

Many tropical islands are only one or two metres above sea level. Scientists think that many of these islands will be underwater in the future because of global warming.

Solids

Like seawater, solids also expand when they are heated. The particles in a substance do not change size when the substance is heated or cooled.

Interesting fact

Water is unusual. It expands instead of contracts as it freezes to become ice.

- When a solid is heated up, its particles vibrate faster. They take up more space and the solid expands.
- When a solid is cooled down, its particles vibrate more slowly. They take up less space and the solid **contracts** or gets smaller.

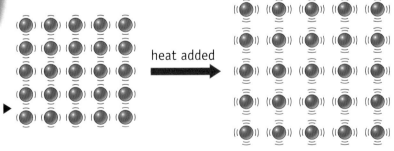

heat added

Particles take up more space ▶ when they are heated but they stay the same size

A **Why do solids expand when they are heated up? (Level 3)**

Different materials expand by different amounts when they are warmed up. Metal tooth fillings expand more than teeth when you have a hot drink. Over time this can make the tooth crack.

Scientists have developed new tooth-coloured materials that expand at almost the same rate as teeth. These make fillings that last much longer.

B Give two advantages of the new tooth fillings compared to metal fillings. (Level 4)

Liquids

- When a liquid is heated up, its particles move around each other faster. They take up more space and the liquid expands.
- When a liquid is cooled down, its particles move around more slowly. They take up less space and the liquid contracts.

Thermometers are filled with a liquid such as mercury or alcohol. When it is heated, the liquid expands and moves up the thermometer.

▲ Expansion joints stop bridges being damaged when they expand in the summer

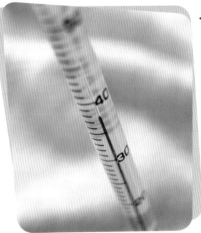

◄ Normal body temperature is about 37 °C

C Explain, using the idea of particles, why the liquid in a thermometer falls when it is cooled. (Level 5)

Gases

Gases also take up more space when they are warmed. Hot air balloons are filled with air heated from a burner. A smaller mass of hot air is needed to fill the balloon than if cold air were used. This makes the total mass of the balloon low enough for the balloon to rise into the air. The height of the balloon above the ground can be controlled by adjusting the temperature of the air inside it.

D Suggest the difficulties that a hot air balloonist might face on very hot days and very cold days. (Level 6)

◄ The container has very cold liquid nitrogen in it

The gas in the balloon ▶ cools and contracts

Keywords
contract, expand

83

3.10 All change!

Learn about:
- what happens when solids melt and liquids evaporate
- what happens when gases condense and liquids freeze

What happens when melted glass is cooled down?

The particles move around more slowly when they are cooled down.

The particles stop moving around when the glass is cold enough.

The particles get joined by forces and the glass turns solid.

▲ Bottles are made by pouring melted glass into a mould and letting it cool

Many substances can exist as solids, liquids and gases. Water is usually a liquid. But cool it down enough and you get ice, a solid. Heat it up enough and you get water vapour, a gas.

Scientists call changes like these **state changes**. Particles do unusual things when a substance changes state.

Melting

Strong forces join the particles in a solid together. The particles can only vibrate and they cannot move around. When a solid is heated up, its particles vibrate faster. If the solid gets hot enough, its particles vibrate so much that some of the forces are overcome. The particles can now move around each other. **Melting** has happened to turn the solid into a liquid.

The temperature at which something changes from a solid to a liquid is called its **melting point**. Different substances have different melting points. Ice melts at 0 °C but iron melts at 1538 °C. The stronger the forces holding the particles together, the higher the melting point.

> A What is meant by the term 'melting point' of a substance? (Level 3)

> B Explain which has the stronger forces between its particles, ice or iron. (Level 4)

Condensing

When a gas is cooled down, its particles move around more slowly. If the gas gets cold enough, its particles move slowly enough for forces to attract them together again. **Condensing** has happened to turn the gas into a liquid.

Evaporating

When a liquid is heated up, its particles move around more quickly. Some particles move around so much that almost all of the forces between them are overcome. The separate particles escape from the surface of the liquid. **Evaporating** has happened to turn some of the liquid into a gas.

The more the liquid is heated, the faster evaporating happens. **Boiling** happens when evaporating takes place throughout the liquid. The temperature at which something boils is called its **boiling point**. The boiling point of a liquid depends on the pressure of the air around it. The lower the pressure, the lower the boiling point.

▲ Boiling water and steam heated by hot rocks underground is thrown into the air by a geyser

C Why do some particles escape from a liquid by evaporating? (Level 5)

D Pressure cookers are used to cook food under high pressure. (i) Explain whether the water in the pressure cooker will boil below or above 100 °C. (ii) Suggest why the water from a geyser can be hotter than 100 °C. (Level 6)

Interesting fact

Water normally boils at 100 °C but on Mount Everest it boils at only 72 °C because the air pressure is lower. Climbers can make tea but it tastes very weak.

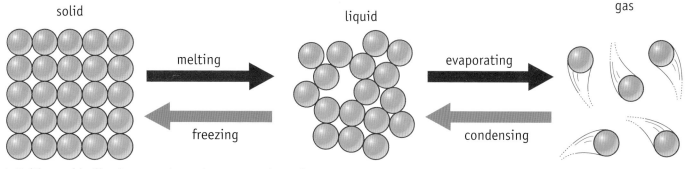

▲ Melting and boiling happen when substances are heated. **Freezing** and condensing happen when substances are cooled.

Keywords
boiling, boiling point, condensing, evaporating, freezing, melting, melting point, state change

3.11 Imagine something unseen

▲ How can you tell that this is a baby elephant?

There is an old story from India. Six men were asked to work out what an elephant is like. But instead of looking at one, they had to touch it in the dark. The man who touched the tail thought it was rope, and the man who touched the trunk thought it was a snake. A tusk was mistaken for a spear, a leg for a tree, and an ear for a fan. The man who touched the elephant's side thought it was a wall.

Each man got a different idea about an elephant. Science can be like this. You can do lots of experiments but you might come to a wrong conclusion.

Are particles real?

You have learned that everything is made of tiny particles. These are so small that you cannot see them. So how can you be sure that they are really there? And if they are there, what are they like? The problem is a bit like the one faced by the men in the dark with the elephant.

A Reach into your pocket or pencil case. Try to identify the objects in there just by touch. For each object, explain how you knew what it was. (Level 3)

Philosophers who lived over 2,000 years ago in Greece thought hard about the world around them. They thought that everything was made of tiny particles, too small to see. They also thought that the particles had different shapes. So a liquid or a gas would be made of rounded particles that flow over each other. A solid would be made of particles with sharp edges.

B **Suggest why the ancient Greeks did not measure the size of their particles. (Level 4)**

C **Do you think the ancient Greeks could be sure that particles have different shapes? (Level 5)**

It is still not possible to see the particles that everything is made from. But scientists have done very many experiments which support the idea that particles exist. They have invented machines that can 'feel' particles.

D **What advantages do scientists today have over the ancient Greek philosophers? (Level 6)**

These are gold particles sitting on a layer of carbon ▶ particles, 'felt' using a special microscope

Interesting fact

If people were the same size as gold particles, everyone in the world would fit into a ball less than a thousandth of a millimetre across.

Bouncing gas particles

Scientists used to have two different ideas about the particles in gases. In one idea, gas particles continually push each other without touching. In the other idea, gas particles continually bounce off each other. Both ideas explained the properties of gases. Ideas like these are called scientific models. They help to explain the things you observe in ways you can understand.

The six men in the Indian story each came up with a different model to explain their observations of an elephant. The model that best explains observations is usually the one that scientists work with. Scientists are always ready to use a different model if someone comes up with a better one.

3 Assess your progress

3.2 A gritty problem

1 What does rock salt contain? (Level 3)
2 Why does seawater taste salty, but tap water does not? (Level 3)
3 Sugar is soluble in water. What does this mean? (Level 4)
4 When powdered chalk is stirred into water, a cloudy white mixture is formed. Is chalk soluble or insoluble in water? (Level 5)
5 Describe an experiment you could carry out to show that rock salt is not as pure as table salt. (Level 6)

3.3 What's the solution?

1 Make a list of the things you can do to speed up dissolving. (Level 3)
2 What do these 's' words mean: solvent, solute, solution, saturated? (Level 3)
3 120 g of sugar is dissolved in 100 g of hot water. What mass of sugar solution forms? (Level 4)
4 No more than 36 g of salt will dissolve in $100\,cm^3$ of water. Alex decides to mix 50 g of salt with $100\,cm^3$ of water. How much salt will *not* dissolve? What is the salt solution called? (Level 5)
5 Kathryn wants to do an experiment to see how quickly sugar cubes and sugar grains dissolve. She knows she should use the same mass of sugar in her experiment. What else must she keep the same to make it a fair test? (Level 6)

3.4 Go with the flow

1 What are the three states of matter? (Level 3)
2 Why is it a good idea to put a lid on a cup of coffee before carrying it? (Level 3)

3 Make a summary table to describe the arrangement and movement of particles in solids, liquids and gases. (Level 4)
4 Why can natural gas for cooking and heating be delivered to homes through pipes? (Level 5)
5 Use the idea of particles to explain why liquids and gases flow freely. (Level 6)

3.6 Mind the gap

1 Name the solute and the solvent in a copper sulfate solution (Level 3)
2 Which substance in a solution of sand, salt and water gets trapped by filter paper? (Level 3)
3 Why can you separate dried peas from dried rice using a sieve? (Level 4)
4 If a cup of dried peas is mixed with a cup of dried rice, the mixture you get is less than 2 cups in volume. Suggest why this happens. (Level 5)
5 Use the idea of particles to explain what happens to an instant coffee granule when it is added to hot water. (Level 6)

3.7 Building bridges

1 Which state of matter (solid, liquid or gas) can change its volume and shape? (Level 3)
2 Which state of matter (solid, liquid or gas) keeps the same volume and shape? (Level 3)
3 Air and water can both change their shape. Suggest why car and bike tyres are filled with air and not with water. (Level 4)
4 Use the idea of particles to explain why a chair can hold your weight without being squashed. (Level 5)
5 You can squash a balloon filled with air. Hannah thought that this can happen because air particles are squashy. Is she correct? Explain your answer. (Level 6)

3.8 Stinky stinks

1 Why can you smell a gas leak when you are in a different room? (Level 3)
2 Where is diffusion likely to be quickest? Choose from a bath of hot water, a hot air balloon and an ice cube. (Level 3)
3 Why does diffusion not happen in solids? (Level 4)
4 Essie dropped a cup half full of orange juice into the washing-up water and went to watch television. Explain why the washing-up water was pale orange when she returned later. (Level 5)
5 Sharks can smell blood half a kilometre away. Explain why the shark might smell blood faster in warm tropical seas than in cold seas. (Level 6)

3.9 Growing in the heat

1 **a** Why can a steel rod fit into a small hole if the rod is first cooled down? **b** Why will the rod get stuck in the hole when the rod warms up again? (Level 3)
2 You can store food in a plastic container in the fridge. What happens to the air in the container as it cools down? (Level 3)
3 Suggest why an oven door is not exactly the same size as the opening to the oven. (Level 4)
4 Concorde was a supersonic airliner built by Britain and France. It flew so fast that it warmed up during flights. Suggest why a gap opened up between a control panel and the wall on Concorde's flight deck during flight. (Level 5)
5 Using the idea of particles, explain why hot air balloons get smaller as the air inside them cools down. (Level 6)

3.10 All change!

1 The melting point of ice is 0 °C. In what state is it: **a** at 25 °C? **b** at −10 °C? (Level 3)
2 Explain what these words mean: melting, evaporating, condensing, freezing. (Level 3)
3 Air contains water vapour. Water vapour is separate particles of water. Why do droplets of water form on cold windows? (Level 4)
4 If you put wet washing outside on a washing line, it soon dries. Martin thought that this was because the heat from the Sun boiled the water in the clothes. Was he right or wrong? Explain your answer. (Level 5)
5 The boiling point of a substance is always higher than its melting point. Explain this observation using the idea of particles and the forces between them. (Level 6)

3.11 Imagine something unseen

1 Which of the two models of gases described on page 87 is used today?
2 What could the men in the Indian story on page 86 have done to collect accurate evidence about the elephant? (Level 4)
3 Why do scientists use models? (Level 5)
4 Suggest why the designers of large buildings use models to check their designs before building work starts. (Level 6)

4.1 Acid attack!

Acids are useful chemicals, but they can also be dangerous.

A tanker carrying a concentrated acid has crashed and acid has poured onto the road. Firefighters arrive quickly in protective clothing to clear the area and deal with the spill. They need to keep people safe but they must also be careful themselves.

- What information about his cargo do you think the driver should know before he sets off?

- Give some examples of warning labels you have seen on bottles and packets, and write down why you think the warnings are there.

- What different types of protective clothing are the firefighters in the picture wearing?

Coming up in this Chapter ...

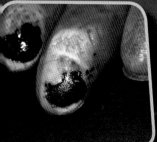

4.2 Dangerous stuff

Learn about:
• the warning signs used on hazardous substances

Small children do not know which substances are dangerous ▲

Interesting fact

Epoxyethane is used to make fibres for clothing and antifreeze for car engines. It is an important chemical but it is difficult to make. Epoxyethane is **toxic** and explodes if it comes into contact with air.

Would you let a small child play with a bottle of bleach or some garden chemicals? Not if you were being responsible. It is often difficult to know whether a substance is safe to handle. Even if you think that the substance might be dangerous, you may not know how to handle it safely or what to do if things go wrong. This is where **hazard warning signs** help.

Hazard warning signs

You will use lots of unfamiliar substances in the laboratory at school. You should assume that everything is dangerous.

You should never taste anything in the lab or fiddle about with equipment and chemicals.

Your teacher will show you how to work safely because they understand the dangers.

You should follow your teacher's instructions, especially when it comes to wearing safety glasses.

Hazardous chemicals come in containers with hazard warning labels on. These often have a yellow or orange background, but they do not have to. The picture on the next page shows four common labels and what they mean.

TOXIC
poisonous substance that can cause death

CORROSIVE
attacks and destroys living tissue, such as skin and eyes

HARMFUL
can make you ill if breathed in, swallowed or absorbed

IRRITANT
can cause red or blistered skin

A What does the skull and crossbones sign mean? (Level 3)

B Why should you treat all chemicals in the lab as dangerous? (Level 4)

Lab hazards

If you spill anything in the laboratory, always tell your teacher straightaway.

- **Corrosive** chemicals are very dangerous. The school technicians will mix them with lots of water to make them safer for you to use.
- **Harmful** or **irritant** chemicals are safer but you still need to take care.

C Explain how corrosive substances can be made safer to use. (Level 5)

Risk assessments

The dangers of a chemical must be balanced against the benefits of using it. Manufacturers use sulfuric acid to make fertilisers. Sulfuric acid is a dangerous chemical, but fertilisers are needed to produce enough food for people to eat.

Your teacher assesses each experiment you do. They work out how to keep any risks as small as possible, and what to do if there is an accident. You will learn how to do this too. Everyone who uses hazardous chemicals, not just scientists, has to carry out risk assessments.

D Petrol is easily set on fire. Suggest some precautions that a petrol station should take. (Level 6)

Transporting chemicals

Road tankers carrying hazardous chemicals carry Hazchem Code labels. These have the correct hazard sign and a code that tells the emergency services what to do if there is an accident. The signs and code have been agreed internationally.

This is important because the people on the scene are unlikely to be scientists and the tanker could be foreign. The accident could be made worse if the emergency services just guessed what to do.

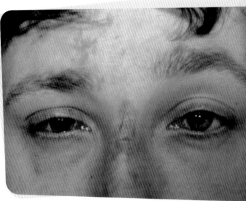

▲ Avoid damage like this by keeping your safety glasses on

▲ This Hazchem Code label warns that the contents of the tanker are flammable – they could be set on fire

Keywords
corrosive, harmful, hazard warning sign, irritant

4.3 Acid, acid, everywhere

Learn about:
- what acids are like
- where you can find acids around you
- why sulfuric acid is so important

Tomato sauce contains ethanoic acid ▲

There are **acids** all around you, often in surprising places. Your stomach contains hydrochloric acid to help you digest your food. Weak acids have a sharp, sour taste. Think of vinegar. It contains ethanoic acid.

The bubbles in fizzy drinks are caused by carbon dioxide. Some of this gas dissolves in the drink to make carbonic acid. Oranges, lemons and grapefruits have a sharp taste because they contain citric acid. Cola drinks contain phosphoric acid which gives them an even sharper taste.

> **A** How could you tell from its taste that a food contains an acid? (Level 3)

Only the pink stems of rhubarb are safe to eat ▼

Dangerous acids

Acids in food and drink are **dilute** acids. They are mixed with a lot of water to make them safe. But concentrated acids are corrosive. They damage skin and clothing, and must never be tasted or left on your skin. Laboratory acids are corrosive like this.

There are strong acids in some household products too. Toilet cleaners contain phosphoric acid or hydrochloric acid, and rust removers contain oxalic acid.

Rhubarb leaves also contain oxalic acid, which is **toxic**. The stalks contain very much less oxalic acid and are safe to eat.

> **B** Cola drinks and toilet cleaners both contain phosphoric acid. Why is it safe to drink cola but not toilet cleaner? (Level 4)

> **C** Explain why it is acceptable for household cleaners to contain corrosive acids even though they can be hazardous. (Level 5)

Millions of tonnes of acid

Sulfuric acid is very corrosive. It is made in huge amounts, more than any other industrial chemical. The chemical industry in the UK makes over a million tonnes of it every year. This is about 11 litres per person. So why is sulfuric acid so important?

- Car batteries contain sulfuric acid, and it is used in the production of petrol and other fuels.
- Sulfuric acid is used to make detergents, plastic, medicines, explosives, fertilisers, paints and dyes.
- It is also used to make titanium dioxide. This is a white powder used in sunblocks, food colouring, toothpaste, cosmetics and paints.

A country's production of sulfuric acid is related to its general economic success. More is produced when the country is wealthy and doing well.

D Suggest a reason for the link between production of sulfuric acid and economic success. (Level 6)

▲ Fertiliser made from sulfuric acid helps farmers to grow our food

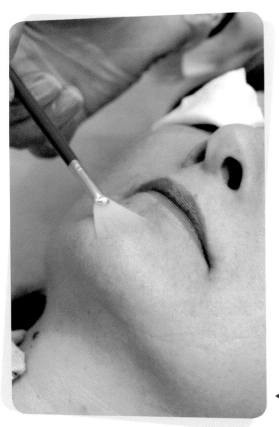

◀ Dilute acids can help to smooth your skin

Science around us

Scientists have developed face peels to smooth the skin and remove some wrinkles. They contain special dilute acids that are safe to use. The peels are applied to the face and remove damaged outer layers of skin.

Keywords
acid, dilute, toxic

4.4 Slippery customers

Learn about:
- the difference between bases and alkalis
- what alkalis are like
- where you can find alkalis around you

If you had been alive over a hundred years ago, you might have cleaned your teeth using charcoal. Luckily today you can choose from all sorts of toothpastes which scientists have developed. They contain powders and detergents to clean your teeth. They also contain sweeteners and flavourings to give a nice taste, and fluoride to help keep tooth decay away.

Toothpastes also contain **bases**. These are the chemical opposites of acids, and they can be just as dangerous.

Toothpaste contains alkalis ▲

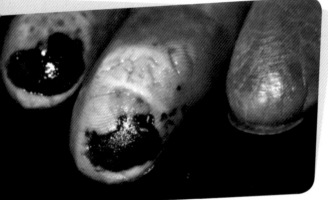
Concentrated alkalis are corrosive and damage skin ▼

Bases and alkalis

Bases are substances that can cancel the acidity of acids so that they become **neutral**. Scientists call the chemical reaction between an acid and a base **neutralisation**. Sodium bicarbonate is used in some toothpastes. It neutralises acids in the mouth that can lead to tooth decay.

Many bases do not dissolve in water. But if a base can dissolve in water, you call it an **alkali**. Most of the bases you come across at school and in everyday life are alkalis. Just like acids, alkalis can be irritant, harmful or corrosive.

A What is neutralisation? (Level 3)

B Why should you handle alkalis carefully? (Level 4)

Alkalis for cleaning

Soap is good at removing dirt. It is made by mixing fats or oils with an alkali, such as sodium hydroxide or potassium hydroxide. Any alkali left in the soap is removed before it is made into bars. This is important because alkalis can damage your skin.

Alkalis feel soapy and slippery. This is because they change the oils on your skin. They make human soap out of you.

C Explain why alkalis feel soapy. (Level 5)

Concentrated alkalis are good at removing grease. They are the main ingredients in many household cleaning products. Sodium hydroxide, sodium carbonate and borax are the alkalis most commonly used. You must wear rubber gloves if you use cleaners for ovens, drains or kitchen surfaces because they are corrosive.

D Chemical hair straightener may contain potassium hydroxide. Suggest why the professional product is allowed to contain more than twice as much potassium hydroxide as the product you can buy to use at home. (Level 6)

▲ These household products all contain alkalis

◄ It is important to change a child's nappy regularly to stop their skin being damaged by ammonia

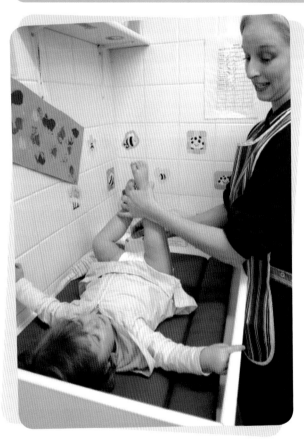

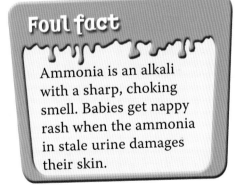

Foul fact

Ammonia is an alkali with a sharp, choking smell. Babies get nappy rash when the ammonia in stale urine damages their skin.

Balanced shampoo

The detergents in shampoo make it slightly **alkaline**. This makes the tiny scales on your strands of hair stand up. They stick together, and your hair looks dull and rough. Shampoo also contains citric acid. This neutralises the alkalis in the shampoo. Just enough citric acid is added so that the shampoo is actually slightly **acidic**. Then the scales lie flat, making the hair look nicer.

Keywords
acidic, alkali, alkaline, base, neutral, neutralisation

4.5 Colour by numbers

Learn about:
- what indicators are and how to use them

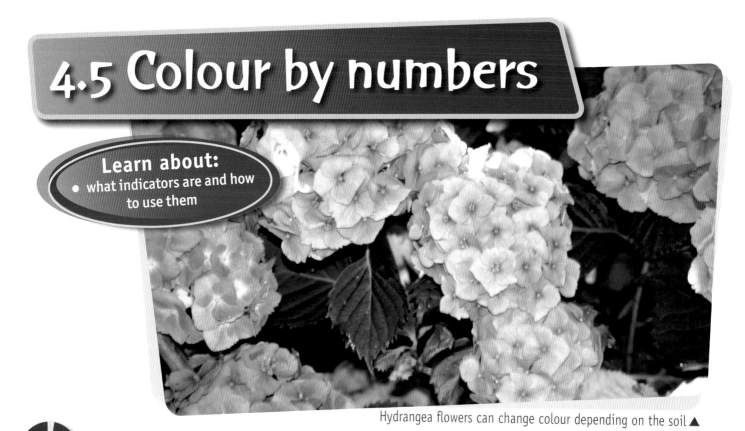

Hydrangea flowers can change colour depending on the soil ▲

Science to the rescue

The pH of aquarium water must be right for the type of fish it contains. Aquarium owners use indicators to check its pH.

There are over seventy kinds of hydrangeas and most of them have white flowers. But some can have different coloured flowers. Their flowers are blue if the plants are growing in an acidic soil, cream in a neutral soil and pink or purple in an alkaline soil.

The coloured substances in the flowers are acting as simple **indicators**. These are chemicals that change colour when added to acids or alkalis. There are lots of these simple indicators and they are really useful.

The litmus test

Litmus is an indicator made from lichen, a type of plant that grows on walls. The colour of litmus paper is different in acids and alkalis. Blue litmus paper turns red in acidic substances. Red litmus paper turns blue in alkaline substances. Neutral substances do not change the colour of litmus paper, except to make it a bit darker because it is damp.

Solution	red litmus paper	blue litmus paper
acidic	stays red	turns red
neutral	stays red	stays blue
alkaline	turns blue	stays blue

▲ Litmus paper tells you whether a substance is acidic, neutral or alkaline

A What colour will blue litmus turn if some acid is added to it? (Level 3)

Universal Indicator

Universal Indicator is a mixture of four different indicators, so it can show a range of colours like a rainbow. Universal Indicator will show you if a substance is acidic, neutral or alkaline. But it will also show you just how strong or weak the acid or alkali is. Universal Indicator comes in the form of paper or a solution.

A colour chart shows you a number on the **pH scale**. This goes from 0 to 14. The pH scale is used by scientists all over the world so they can share information about acids and alkalis.

When you use Universal Indicator paper:
- use a glass rod to add a small spot of the test substance
- wait 30 seconds for the colour to develop
- match the spot's colour to a colour chart.

The Universal Indicator colour chart ▼

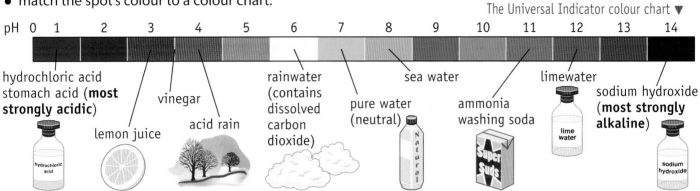

pH 0 1 2 3 4 5 6 7 8 9 10 11 12 13 14

hydrochloric acid stomach acid (**most strongly acidic**)

lemon juice

vinegar

acid rain

rainwater (contains dissolved carbon dioxide)

pure water (neutral)

sea water

ammonia washing soda

limewater

sodium hydroxide (**most strongly alkaline**)

B What colour does Universal Indicator turn in pure water? (Level 4)

Neutral substances are pH7

Acids are less than pH7 and alkalis are more than pH7

Acids are stronger the closer to pH0 you go

Alkalis are stronger the closer to pH14 you go

You only need to add a few drops of Universal Indicator solution to a substance to see if it is acidic, neutral or alkaline ▼

C Why are you unable to use a pH colour chart with litmus paper? (Level 5)

D Normal skin has a pH of about 5.5 – what does this tell you? Suggest an advantage of using 'pH balanced' soap at the same pH. (Level 6)

Keywords
indicator, litmus, pH scale, Universal Indicator

4.6 A base for an ache

Learn about:
- how stomach acid can be neutralised
- how to carry out a neutralisation experiment

Your stomach contains hydrochloric acid. This kills harmful bacteria that might be swallowed with your food. It also helps you to **digest** your food. It would digest you, too, if your stomach did not have a protective layer.

If you scoff your food, you could get indigestion ▲

Foul fact

Your digestive system makes about 8 litres of stomach acid each day. Stomach acid is about pH 2.

If you eat too much food or eat too quickly, you run a risk of getting **indigestion**. This is caused by the hydrochloric acid escaping into the lower part of your throat and stinging it. Medicines called **antacids** can come to your rescue.

How antacids work

When an acid and a base are mixed together, they neutralise each other. Some indigestion remedies contain insoluble bases such as calcium carbonate. Others contain soluble bases, or alkalis, such as magnesium hydroxide or sodium bicarbonate.

> **A** Name an alkali found in antacid tablets. (Level 3)

These are all antacids. They neutralise stomach acid ▼

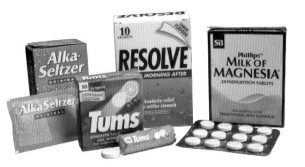

Investigating neutralisation

How much antacid is needed to neutralise some stomach acid? You can carry out an investigation to find out.

It would be a bit tricky to collect someone's stomach acid to test it. You can use laboratory hydrochloric acid instead. The acid will be neutralised if you add enough antacid to it. You can check if this has happened using Universal Indicator. The colour of the indicator will change as more and more antacid is added. At some point you will have added enough antacid to neutralise the acid.

> **B** (i) What colour will the Universal Indicator be when the hydrochloric acid has been neutralised? (ii) What will the pH be? (Level 4)

> Neutralisation reactions can be really useful. Bee stings contain acid. You can take away the pain by putting a base or alkali on the place where you were stung.

> Wasp stings contain a base, so you can treat them with an acid like vinegar.

Testing different antacids

Becca does an experiment to see how much of different antacids will neutralise hydrochloric acid. She sets up five test tubes, each with the same amount of hydrochloric acid and adds Universal Indicator to each test tube. Then Becca dissolves five different antacids in water. She uses a pipette to add each antacid to a test tube of hydrochloric acid until the acid is neutralised. She records her results in a table.

Antacid test results

Name of antacid	Amount needed to neutralise acid (cm³)	Cost per 100 cm³
Acid-away	25 cm³	£1.30
Settletum	20 cm³	£2.20
Neutralise!	15 cm³	£1.60
Morning after	30 cm³	£2.00
Indi-alka	10 cm³	£2.50

▲ Becca could also use a pH probe to check the pH during her investigation

C Why did Becca use the same volume of hydrochloric acid in each test tube? (Level 5)

D Which of the antacids would you recommend to a friend, and why? (Level 6)

Keywords
antacid, digest, indigestion

4.7 Now you see it!

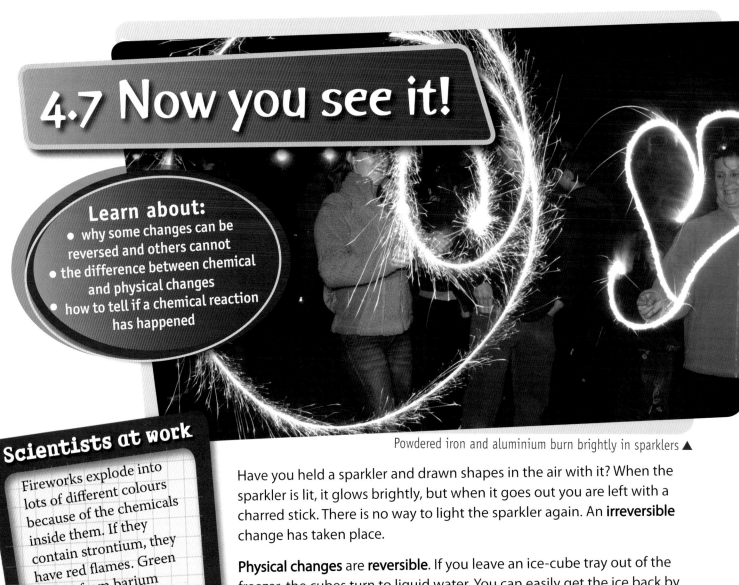

Powdered iron and aluminium burn brightly in sparklers ▲

Scientists at work

Fireworks explode into lots of different colours because of the chemicals inside them. If they contain strontium, they have red flames. Green comes from barium and blue from copper. Fireworks manufacturers need to know which chemical produces which colour.

Have you held a sparkler and drawn shapes in the air with it? When the sparkler is lit, it glows brightly, but when it goes out you are left with a charred stick. There is no way to light the sparkler again. An **irreversible** change has taken place.

Physical changes are **reversible**. If you leave an ice-cube tray out of the freezer, the cubes turn to liquid water. You can easily get the ice back by putting the tray in the freezer again.

> **A** When water boils and becomes steam, has a reversible or an irreversible change taken place? (Level 3)

What is a chemical reaction?

When a **chemical reaction** happens, one or more new substances are made. These are called the **products**. The substances you started with are called the **reactants**. Most chemical reactions are irreversible. Once the products have been made, it is very difficult to turn them back into the original reactants.

It is easy to see that some chemical reactions are happening, such as during a firework display or when baking a cake. Ingredients such as butter, flour, eggs, baking powder and sugar are the reactants for a cake. They are very different from the cake they make.

◄ Gunpowder is used in fireworks. It reacts very quickly when heated up

Chemical reactions often need energy to get them started. They can then give out energy as sound, heat or light. The explosion you hear with big fireworks is the result of a chemical reaction.

> **B** When you light a sparkler, is a chemical reaction or a physical change taking place? (Level 4)

Observing chemical reactions

Becca and Ryan are mixing different substances together in the science lab to see if a chemical reaction has taken place. They mix each pair of substances in a test tube and then heat the test tube over a Bunsen burner. They record their observations in a table.

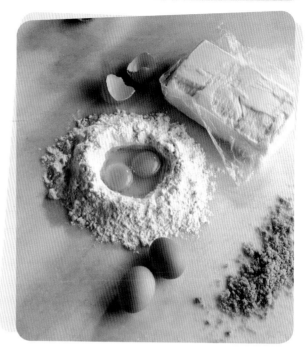

▲ Energy from an oven is needed to turn these reactants into a tasty cake

▼ Iron and sulfur react together to produce iron sulfide. Lots of heat energy is given off in the reaction

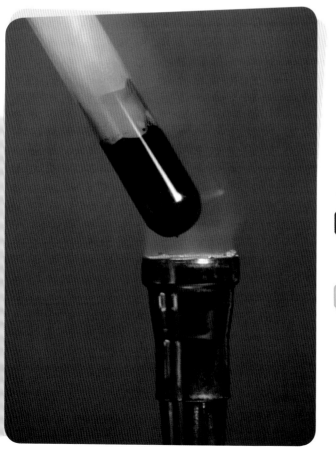

Chemical reaction or physical change

Mixing...	What they see
baking powder and vinegar	Lots of bubbles are given off.
iron powder and sulfur powder	The mixture glows brightly when heated. A grey solid is produced.
sand and water	Sand sinks to the bottom of the water.

> **C** Which two pairs of substances produce a chemical reaction? Explain how you know. (Level 5)

> **D** Describe how you can show that one of the pairs of substances does not produce a chemical reaction. (Level 6)

Keywords
chemical reaction, irreversible, physical change, product, reactant, reversible

4.8 Cars and kettles

Acids can be corrosive! ▲

Jasmine's dad has been having problems with the old car he is doing up. The photo shows the metal tray that his car battery sits on. The acid from the car battery has leaked onto the tray and eaten it away. 'This is going to cost a fortune to replace,' he says to Jasmine.

A Explain how acid has damaged Jasmine's dad's car. (Level 3)

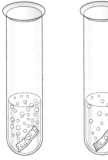    

magnesium   zinc   iron   copper   silver

Which metals react with hydrochloric acid? ▲

Reacting acids with metals

When metals are used up like this in chemical reactions, scientists call it **corrosion**. The diagram shows different metals in hydrochloric acid.

You will see that bubbles appear in some of the test tubes. The pieces of metal get smaller as they react with the acid. Other metals don't react with the acid, so you don't see anything happening.

B How can you tell there is a chemical reaction between zinc and hydrochloric acid? (Level 4)

Testing for hydrogen

The gas given off when a metal reacts with an acid is flammable. This means that it burns. The gas is called **hydrogen**. Hydrogen is one of the products of the reaction.

You can collect hydrogen in an upside-down test tube. The photo shows you how this can be done. Hydrogen pushes the water out of the tube and is collected at the top of the tube.

The reaction between zinc and sulfuric acid produces hydrogen ▼

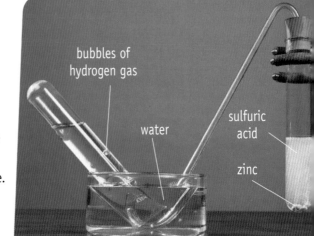

bubbles of hydrogen gas

water

sulfuric acid

zinc

If you take the test tube out of the water and bring a lighted splint near the mouth of the test tube, you hear a squeaky pop as the hydrogen burns.

Reacting acids with carbonates

In the kitchen, Jasmine's mum is working on her laptop. She asks Jasmine to make her a cup of tea. Jasmine takes the lid off the kettle, ready to fill it up from the kitchen tap. 'Yuk,' she says, as she sees the grey furry stuff inside. Her mum takes a look. 'The kettle has got **limescale** inside it.' 'Limescale is calcium carbonate, which is a base,' says Jasmine.

Jasmine's mum fetches a bottle of limescale remover. 'We need to put this in the kettle to get rid of the limescale,' she says, and pours some into the kettle. Jasmine and her mum see bubbles fizzing away in the kettle.

▲ How to test for hydrogen

> **C** Limescale is a base. Limescale removers usually contain acid. What kind of reaction takes place when limescale removers react with acid? (Level 5)

Pollution in the air makes rainwater acidic. This is called **acid rain**. Limestone and marble are rocks made from calcium carbonate.
These rocks react with acid rain and are slowly used up. Because we use limestone and marble to make buildings and statues, acid rain can be a problem as it reacts with the rocks.

Interesting fact

The Sphinx is a famous Egyptian statue. Its face is disappearing because the rock it is made from is reacting with acids in rain water, and in water vapour in the air.

The test for carbon dioxide

There are lots of different **carbonates**. When acids react with carbonates, bubbles of **carbon dioxide** gas are given off. You can test whether carbon dioxide is given off in a reaction by bubbling the gas through **limewater**. If the gas is carbon dioxide, it will turn the limewater milky.

▲ Limewater turns milky white when carbon dioxide is bubbled through it

> **D** Carbon dioxide dissolves to form an acid solution. The milky white colour in limewater is caused by calcium carbonate. Suggest why milky limewater goes clear again if a lot of carbon dioxide is bubbled through it. (Level 6)

Keywords
acid rain, carbon dioxide, carbonate, corrosion, hydrogen, limescale, limewater

4.9 Fire alarm!

Learn about:
- what fires are
- why things burn
- how to put out fires

A forest fire at night ▲

People all over the world still cook over an open fire ▼

Every summer a forest fire breaks out somewhere. A small spark or a carelessly dropped match is often all it takes. The bushes and trees are dry and are easily set alight. As the fire rages on, it burns everything in its path. Animals die if they cannot run or fly away. Meanwhile, the firefighters hope for rain. They know that without it, they might need days or weeks to bring the fire under control.

Burning

Burning is a chemical reaction. It is often called **combustion**. Particles in the **fuel** join with **oxygen** particles from the air. This makes new substances and releases energy. You can feel the thermal energy from a fire. The substances coming from the fire get so hot that they give off light energy. They glow. This is why you can see flames.

Combustion is very useful. The thermal energy from burning fuels keeps you warm in winter and cooks your food. It is used to make electricity at power stations.

A Name two ways in which energy is released in a fire. (Level 3)

The fire triangle

Fires need three things to start and keep burning. They need oxygen from the air, thermal energy and a fuel. These are shown in the **fire triangle**. You cannot start a fire without thermal energy. Once a fire has started, it releases more thermal energy. This lights the next bit of fuel and the fire keeps going.

The fire triangle ▲

B Explain what fires need to start and keep burning. (Level 4)

Fighting fires

A fire will go out if you break the fire triangle. So there are three ways you can put out a fire. You can take away:

- the oxygen
- the **thermal energy**
- the fuel.

Fire blankets stop the air getting to a fire. The oxygen under the blanket gets used up and the fire goes out. Powder extinguishers coat the fire with powder, stopping oxygen getting to it. Carbon dioxide fire extinguishers replace the air around the fire with carbon dioxide. The carbon dioxide is also very cold, so it takes the thermal energy away. Water fire extinguishers take the thermal energy away too.

C **Fires can be put out using a layer of foam. Suggest how foam puts out a fire. (Level 5)**

Firefighters may cut down a line of trees in a forest fire. The fire runs out of fuel when it reaches the gap in the trees, so it goes out.

D Visitors to a forest noticed something strange. On one side of the road there were lots of leafy trees but on the other side there were only burned remains. Suggest what has happened. (Level 6)

Water takes away the thermal energy from a fire and puts it out ▼

▲ A fire blanket smothers the flames of a fire

Scientists at work

Fire researchers investigate the best ways to put out fires. They carry out experiments and analyse the causes of fires to make buildings as safe as possible.

Keywords
combustion, fire triangle, fuel, oxygen, thermal energy

4.10 What's in an acid?

Learn about:
- how ideas about acids have changed through time

◄ Gold is a very valuable metal. It does not normally react with acids

People have been interested in how the world works for thousands of years. But the word 'scientist' was only invented in 1833. Before then, scientists were called natural philosophers.

Centuries ago, alchemists studied chemical reactions. One of the things that interested them was gold. They believed that acids could help them to make gold from ordinary metals.

Aqua regia

Alchemists knew about sulfuric acid and nitric acid as early as the ninth century. Then in the fourteenth century an Iranian alchemist called Jabir ibn Hayyan mixed table salt with sulfuric acid. A reaction gave off fumes with a sharp, choking smell. These dissolved in water to make hydrochloric acid.

Jabir discovered that very concentrated hydrochloric acid and nitric acid made a mixture which was so powerful it could dissolve gold. The mixture was called 'aqua regia', which means 'royal water'.

A | **What is aqua regia made from?** (Level 3)

Jabir ibn Hayyan did careful experiments and invented some laboratory equipment ▼

The acid maker

In the past, no one was really sure what different substances were made from. Many substances had lots of different names. Hydrochloric acid was called spirit of salt or muriatic acid.

A French chemist called Antoine Lavoisier was one of the people who discovered oxygen in 1774. He gave oxygen its name, which means 'acid maker'. His experiments with oxygen led him to think that all acids contain oxygen.

> **B** Suggest why hydrochloric acid used to be called spirit of salt. (Level 4)

◄ Sulfur burns in oxygen to make an acidic gas

> A formula shows what a chemical contains. For example, O stands for oxygen and H stands for hydrogen.

Testing times

In science, lots of experiments can only support an idea. No matter how many you do, you cannot actually prove that a scientific idea is right. But it takes only one experiment to show that an idea is wrong.

Lavoisier thought that acids were acids because they contained oxygen. If any acid could be found that did not contain oxygen, his idea would be proved wrong. The table shows some acids and their chemical formulas.

Name of acid	Chemical formula
Nitric acid	HNO_3
Sulfuric acid	H_2SO_4
Phosphoric acid	H_3PO_4

> **C** Look at the table and suggest why Lavoisier might have been right that acids are acids because they contain oxygen. (Level 5)

In 1818, Sir Humphry Davy showed that hydrochloric acid contains only hydrogen and chlorine. Its formula is HCl. This showed that Lavoisier was wrong and a new idea about acids was needed.

> **D** Look again at the acids in the table and the formula of hydrochloric acid. What do they really all have in common? (Level 6)

4 Assess your progress

4.2 Dangerous stuff

1 Draw the hazard warning sign for an irritant. (Level 3)

2 Explain what these words mean: corrosive, harmful, irritant. (Level 3)

3 What is the difference between a toxic substance and a harmful one? (Level 4)

4 Suggest why hazard warning signs are used on labels instead of written warnings. (Level 5)

5 A household cleaning product is supplied in a spray can. It carries the hazard symbols for 'irritant' and 'flammable'. Describe the precautions you should take when using it. (Level 6)

4.3 Acid, acid everywhere

1 Name three acids found in food or drink. (Level 3)

2 Name three acids found in household products. (Level 3)

3 Why should you wear rubber gloves when you use rust remover? (Level 4)

4 You can rub rhubarb on pans to make them shiny again. Suggest why this might work. (Level 5)

5 Substances added to food and drink are given 'E numbers'. E513 is very dilute sulfuric acid. Sulfuric acid is 'schwefelsäure' in German, 'zwavelzuur' in Dutch and 'acido solforico' in Italian. Give two reasons why E numbers are important. (Level 6)

4.4 Slippery customers

1 What do you call a base that can dissolve in water? (Level 3)

2 Name an alkali. (Level 3)

3 Describe how soap is made. (Level 4)

4 Some books about cleaning suggest using sodium bicarbonate solution as a household cleaning product. Why should this work? (Level 5)

5 Toothpaste may contain sodium hydroxide. Explain why it is an ingredient, and why it is present in only tiny amounts. (Level 6)

4.5 Colour by numbers

1 What colour will red litmus turn if some alkali is added to it? (Level 3)

2 What colour is Universal Indicator in a neutral solution? (Level 3)

3 Charlie added a few drops of liquid to two pieces of litmus paper. The red litmus paper stayed red and the blue litmus paper stayed blue. Was the liquid acidic, alkaline or neutral? (Level 4)

4 When Yasmine added a few drops of a liquid to red litmus paper, it stayed red. She thought that the liquid was an acid. Explain why Yasmine might have been wrong. (Level 5)

5 Give two reasons why Universal Indicator is more useful than litmus paper. (Level 6)

4.6 A base for an ache

1 Name the acid found in your stomach. (Level 3)

2 What is an antacid? (Level 3)

3 Explain how you could check the pH of a sample of stomach acid. (Level 4)

4 Some antacids produce carbon dioxide gas when they react with stomach acid. What problem might this cause? (Level 5)

5 Describe what would happen if bee sting and wasp sting were mixed together. Explain your answer. (Level 6)

4.7 Now you see it!

1 State a difference between a chemical reaction and a physical change. (Level 3)

2 Name a metal used in sparklers. (Level 3)

3 Magnesium oxide is made when magnesium burns in air. Name one reactant and one product of this reaction. (Level 4)

4 Give **three** reasons why burning a match involves chemical reactions. (Level 5)

5 Explain how you know that cooking, such as frying an egg or baking a cake, involves chemical reactions. (Level 6)

4.8 Cars and kettles

1 In the experiment on page 104, how can you tell that silver does not react with hydrochloric acid? (Level 3)

2 What happens when a lighted splint is put near the mouth of a test tube of hydrogen gas? (Level 3)

3 Suggest why gold is used for teeth fillings. (Level 4)

4 Why do you think that limescale remover contains a weak acid and not a strong acid? (Level 5)

5 Explain how you could check if bubbles of a gas contain hydrogen or carbon dioxide. Include what you would do, and what you would observe. (Level 6)

4.9 Fire alarm!

1 Name **one** way to put out a fire. (Level 3)

2 Where does the oxygen for a fire usually come from? (Level 3)

3 Explain why you must strike a match against a rough surface to get it to light. (Level 4)

4 Oil floats on water. Explain why you should put out a cooking oil fire using a fire blanket or damp cloth, rather than with water. (Level 5)

5 Use the fire triangle to explain why each of these firefighting methods works: **a** spraying a fine mist of water; **b** using a carbon dioxide fire extinguisher. (Level 6)

4.10 What's in an acid?

1 Give two old names for hydrochloric acid. (Level 3)

2 Look at page 109. Why did Lavoisier give oxygen its name? (Level 4)

3 Explain why hydrochloric acid was important in changing scientists' ideas about acids. (Level 5)

4 Acids give particles of hydrogen to other substances. The more particles of hydrogen acids can give away, the stronger they are. Which acid in the table on page 109 might be the strongest acid? Give a reason for your answer. (Level 6)

Feel the force

Forces are all around you. Without forces, nothing would move and you would not be able to get to school or go to the circus.

Without forces, the cannon in the picture could not fire, the trapeze artist could not hold on and the seesaw would not work. Forces make things move and make things happen – imagine a life without forces!

- What units are forces measured in?

- What sort of force is used in a tug of war?

- Write down some examples in everyday life where forces are used.

Coming up in this Chapter ...

5.2 A weight problem

Learn about:
- the difference between mass and weight
- how you can measure weight

Go to the Moon for instant weight loss ▲

Some people worry about their **weight**. They try to lose weight by dieting. But there is another way to lose weight … take a trip to the Moon! It works for everyone. Whatever you weigh on Earth, you will weigh six times less on the Moon.

Right now the Earth's **gravity** is pulling you towards the centre of the planet. You don't fall to the Earth's core because the ground is in the way. It supports your weight. Weight is a **force** that can act at a distance. It tells you how much the Earth's gravity is pulling you towards its centre. Another example of a force acting at a distance is **magnetism**. Other forces, such as **friction,** need objects to be in contact with each other for the forces to affect them. These are called **contact forces**.

A Explain what weight is. (Level 3)

B Write down one example of a contact force and two forces that act at a distance. (Level 4)

Weight and mass

Interesting fact

An astronaut on the Moon weighs about the same as a watermelon weighs on Earth.

Sam buys a massive bar of chocolate. If he takes it to the Moon, it will still be massive – its **mass** will stay the same as its mass on the Earth. An object's mass is constant. It depends on how much matter it has. The weight of the chocolate bar depends on the gravity of the object it is near, such as a planet or a moon.

People often use the word 'weight' when a scientist would say mass. When someone says they weigh 50 **kilograms,** then scientifically speaking they mean that their mass is 50 kg.

Weight is a force, measured in **newtons** (N). On Earth, a person with a mass of 50 kg pushes down on the ground with a force – or weight – of about 500 newtons. If you know an object's mass in kilograms, you can find its weight approximately by multiplying by 10.

If a bag of potatoes has a mass of 2 kg, its weight on Earth would be 20 N. If you took these potatoes to the Moon then their mass would still be 2 kg, but their weight would only be about 3 N. This is because the gravity on the Moon is only about a sixth of the gravity on Earth.

> If I took this massive bar of chocolate to the Moon it would still be just as massive – its mass would stay the same. But its weight would decrease because the gravity on the Moon is less.

C What is the weight of an object with a mass of 23 kg on the Earth? (Level 5)

Different places, different weights

	On Earth	On the Moon	In outer space	Near Neptune
Mass (kg)	35	35	35	35
Weight (N)	350	59	0	394

D Jupiter has more mass than the Earth. How do you think your weight would change if you went there? Explain your answer. (Level 6)

Measuring weight

You can use a spring balance or a force meter to measure the weight of an object. When you hang an object from a force meter it extends the spring – the longer the extension, the greater the object's weight.

Before   **After**

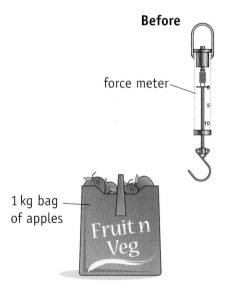

force meter

1 kg bag of apples

▲ A 1 kg bag of apples weighs 10 N

The apples weigh 10 N

Keywords
contact force, friction gravity, kilogram, magnetism, mass, newton, weight

5.3 Friction: friend and foe!

Learn about:
- when friction is useful and when it is not
- reducing friction
- the science of tyres

Sprinting to the finish ▲

Tour de France cyclists are very fit. But even the fittest cyclist would not win without a well-maintained bike. To keep a racing bike in top condition, you need to know all about friction.

Friction and bicycles

Friction is a force that acts when surfaces rub together. It can be a useful force. Friction between a bike's tyres and the road give it grip. When you apply your brakes, friction slows you down. But sometimes friction is not useful.

Friction causes problems when two surfaces rub together. One problem is that the parts are worn away. Friction also creates heat which is often wasted energy. To reduce friction we use lubricants such as oils and grease.

▲ These stone steps have been worn away by the friction of shoes

A What problems does friction cause? (Level 3)

Scientists at work

Shoe designers have to think about friction as well. They have to choose a material for the soles of shoes that looks good and stops people slipping over.

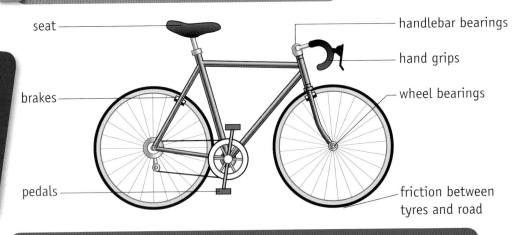

seat — handlebar bearings — hand grips — wheel bearings — brakes — pedals — friction between tyres and road

B Look at the diagram of the bike. Make two lists from the parts labelled, one list for 'Useful friction' and the other for 'Not useful friction'. (Level 4)

Choosing the right tyre

An F1 racing car comes smoothly round the last bend and down the final straight. Fans cheer as it passes the chequered flag. Friction between its tyres and the road gives it the grip it needs to take corners so fast. There are several types of tyre to choose from.

'Wet' racing tyres have grooves cut into them like ordinary car tyres, so they can get rid of water, but they slow the car down. 'Dry' tyres have the most grip but cannot get rid of the water when it rains. Intermediate tyres are in the middle. They can get rid of a little water and are faster than wet tyres on a damp track.

F1 cars need friction to hug the bends ▲

'dry' tyres

'wet' tyres

'intermediate' tyres

F1 tyres ▲

C **Look at the diagram of the 'dry' tyre. Why do you think it cannot get rid of water? (Level 5)**

The table shows the average lap times for a racing car on a track using the different types of tyre.

Why grooves are important ▼

Racing car average lap times

Tyre type	Average lap time (seconds)		
	Dry weather	Damp weather	Wet weather
'Dry'	45	90	100
'Intermediate'	60	70	90
'Wet'	80	75	70

D Using the table, suggest the best tyres to use in the following weather situations: **(i)** a 10-lap race on a dry sunny day, **(ii)** a 10-lap race which starts dry but rain is forecast after five laps. (Level 6)

5.4 Battle of the forces

Learn about:
- balanced and unbalanced forces
- what happens when unbalanced forces act on objects

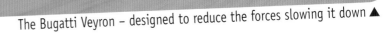
The Bugatti Veyron – designed to reduce the forces slowing it down ▲

Interesting fact

The Bugatti Veyron cost £250,000,000 to design and build, and the company will make only 300 cars. That's why they cost £840,000 each!

The average car has around 100 hp (horsepower) and does 180 kph (kilometres per hour). The Bugatti Veyron has 1000 hp and does 400 kph. For a car to move that fast, you have to overcome lots of forces.

Showing forces

All the objects in the picture have forces acting on them. A force is something which changes the speed and/or direction of movement of an object.

> Scientists use arrows to show the forces acting on an object. The longer the arrow, the greater the force and the greater the change in speed and/or direction.

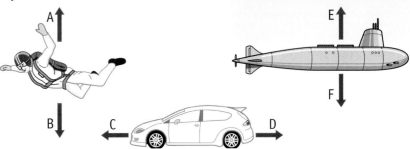
Forces are shown by arrows ▲

A Can you name the forces in the picture above? Choose from the following: air resistance, upthrust, weight, engine force. (Level 3)

Balanced forces

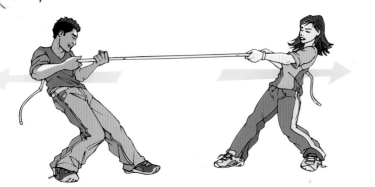

Tina and Alex are having a tug of war. They are not moving. They are pulling with the same sized force, but in opposite directions. We say the forces are **balanced forces**. This means the forces cancel each other out.

The diagram shows a car travelling at a speed of 13 m/s. The speed and direction of the car are not changing, so the forces on the car are balanced. They cancel each other out. There is no overall force acting to change the speed or direction.

engine force 500 N

air resistance

B Look at the diagram of the car. How big is the air resistance force? (Level 4)

A

Unbalanced forces

The diagram of cars A and B shows **unbalanced forces** on the two cars. You can tell that the forces are unbalanced because one arrow is longer than the other.

B

- If the larger force is in the same direction as the car is moving, then the car will speed up.
- If the larger force is in the opposite direction to the moving car, then the car will slow down.

If another car crashed into car A from the side, then the force would change car A's direction and its shape as it would be crushed.

C In the diagram, what would happen to the speeds of cars A and B? (Level 5)

Forces adding together

When two forces act in the same direction, they can combine together to make a bigger force. The small boat in the picture has an engine and a sail. These forces combine to give a total force of 150 N.

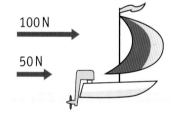

100 N

50 N

Forging steel ▼

D What affects the size of the air resistance acting on a moving car? (Level 6)

Forces in action

Unbalanced forces can do more to an object than change its speed and direction. The photo shows a forge. A piece of steel called a billet is placed at the bottom, and a very large piece of metal called a die is dropped on it, changing the billet's shape.

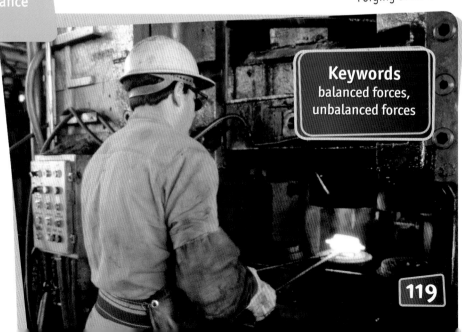

Keywords
balanced forces,
unbalanced forces

5.5 Speeding up and slowing down

Learn about:
- how to measure speed
- how to drive safely

A pile-up on the motorway ▲

Cars allow you to get around the country quickly. But they are dangerous machines with large forces acting on them. The Highway Code tells you the **stopping distances** for cars at different **speeds**. You should not drive closer than this to the car in front.

If you ignore this advice, serious accidents can happen. Around 3500 people are killed in road accidents in the UK every year.

Measuring speed

To find the speed of an object, you need to know the distance it travels and the time it takes to travel that distance. The equation shows how we calculate speed.

$$\text{speed (m/s)} = \frac{\text{distance (m)}}{\text{time (s)}}$$

m = metres
s = seconds

Interesting fact

In 2004, NASA's X-43A unmanned aircraft reached a speed of 11,270 km/h. That's fast!

Look at the table showing the distances and times taken by four runners. Answer the questions, using the equation above if necessary.

Running distances and times

Runner	Distance (m)	Time (s)
Angus	80	20
Ali	45	10
Emma	60	6
Sarah	200	40

A Who ran the furthest? (Level 3)   **B** Who ran the slowest? (Level 4)

Stopping distances

Drivers need to be able to stop their car without crashing into the car in front. The distance it takes them to stop is called the stopping distance.

When a driver decides to stop, it takes time to step on the brakes. The car is still travelling at the same speed while this happens. This is the **thinking distance**. The thinking distance the car travels depends on how alert the driver is.

> **C** Can you think of anything that would make the driver less alert than normal? (Level 5)

Scientists at work

Specialist police officers can work out the speed of a car before a crash by measuring the tyre tracks. This tells them the braking distance of the car.

◄ Accidents often happen when drivers don't leave enough stopping distance

After the driver pushes the brake pedal, the car slows down. It continues to travel until it stops. This is called the **braking distance**.

The total stopping distance is the thinking distance plus the braking distance. The diagram shows the stopping distances in the Highway Code.

Typical stopping distances ▼

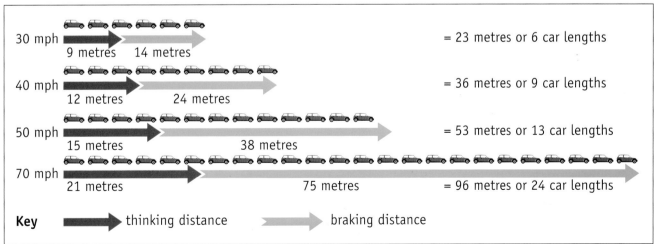

30 mph	9 metres 14 metres	= 23 metres or 6 car lengths
40 mph	12 metres 24 metres	= 36 metres or 9 car lengths
50 mph	15 metres 38 metres	= 53 metres or 13 car lengths
70 mph	21 metres 75 metres	= 96 metres or 24 car lengths

Key ➤ thinking distance ➤ braking distance

> **D** How much further will a car move before stopping if it is travelling at 40 mph than if it is travelling at 30 mph? (Level 6)

Keywords
braking distance, speed, stopping distance, thinking distance

5.6 Investigating falling objects

Learn about:
- how scientific ideas develop
- the importance of experimentation

I think that heavy objects fall to the Earth more quickly than light objects.

Aristotle was born around 2,500 years ago. He was an important thinker and was very influential for centuries after his death. He had ideas on many subjects, one of which was objects falling to the ground.

What would Aristotle think?

▲ Which objects fall the quickest?

A If the shelf broke, put the objects in the order in which you think they would hit the ground. (Level 3)

B Explain why you put them in this order. (Level 4)

Aristotle would have said the heaviest object would hit the ground first, then the second heaviest and so on, until the lightest object hit the ground last. Perhaps you did the same.

Aristotle thought about things like this and came up with theories. He did not do experiments. This was how science was done in ancient Greece. His theory about falling objects was that the heavier an object, the faster it falls. So if two objects have the same weight they would fall at the same speed.

C What do you think Aristotle would say happens if you drop two identical pieces of paper, one crumpled up and the other flat? (Level 5)

To check your answer try the experiment with the paper. What did you find out? You've probably proved the great Aristotle wrong – not bad for Year 7!

Galileo's experiments

If you drop two objects with the same shape and size, they will hit the ground at the same time.

Galileo experimented by dropping balls from the Leaning Tower of Pisa ▼

Galileo was an Italian scientist who was born in 1564. He did experiments to test his ideas. He realised that heavy objects do not always fall the fastest, so he looked for a reason.

Galileo's idea was that air resistance, which is the friction between falling objects and the air, decides if one object falls more quickly than another.

The story goes that he made two balls, one very heavy and one light. They were the same shape and size. He dropped them from the top of the Leaning Tower of Pisa. Both balls hit the ground at the same time. This proved that Aristotle's theory was wrong. Scientific ideas can change like this as new evidence becomes available.

D · There is no air on the Moon. If you repeated the paper experiment on the Moon, what do you think would happen? Explain your answer. (Level 6)

Interesting fact

Galileo was jailed for life by the Catholic Church, just for saying that the Earth moved around the Sun.

A theory is a set of ideas that explains something. Scientists nowadays often do experiments to prove whether a theory is right or not. But not all theories can be checked by doing experiments.

5 Assess your progress

5.2 A weight problem

1 Copy and complete the sentences using these words:
weight   mass   newtons   kilograms

The _____ of an object is constant and depends on the amount of matter it has. Gravity gives an object its _____ . Mass is measured in _____ . Weight is a force and is measured in _____ . (Level 3)

2 If you went to the Moon, how would your weight and mass change? (Level 3)

3 How do you think the Sun's gravity compares with the Earth's? Explain your answer. (Level 4)

4 Rank these objects in terms of the amount of gravity they have: Earth, Sun, pencil sharpener, Moon, Jupiter. (Level 5)

5 Michelle says 'If you go to the Moon, you'll be slimmer because you lose weight'. Do you think she is right or wrong? Explain your answer. (Level 6)

5.3 Friction: friend and foe!

1 How can we reduce the amount of friction on moving parts? (Level 3)

2 Copy and complete the sentences using these words: **brakes   surfaces   worn**

Friction is caused when two _____ rub together. It is useful when we want to use our _____ . When two _____ rub together, friction causes them to be _____ down. (Level 3)

3 Why are you much more likely to crash when riding a bike on an icy day? (Level 4)

4 Why do cars that go off-road have deeper grooves cut into their tyres than road cars? (Level 5)

5 Why does a racing car with 'wet' tyres travel more slowly in dry weather than one with 'dry' tyres? (Level 6)

5.4 Battle of the forces

1 What three things can happen to an object if the forces acting on it are unbalanced? (Level 3)

2 Copy and complete the sentences using these words:
constant   length   balanced   directions   st

When two forces are equal in size but opposite in direction, they are called _____ forces. If the forces on an object are balanced, it will stay _____ or mov at a _____ speed. If forces are balanced, force arrow will be the same _____ but point in opposite _____ (Level 3)

3 a Use a force arrow diagram to show a radio-controll car moving with a force of 3 N, with a friction force of 1 N. Use a scale of 1 cm = 1 N. b Are these forces combining or cancelling each other? (Level 4)

4 If a car is speeding up and the engine force is 250 N what can you say about the size of the air resistance and friction? (Level 5)

5 Why can the weight of a car and its engine force nev be balanced? (Level 6)

5.5 Speeding up and slowing down

1 Copy and complete the sentences using these
words: **distance   metres   time   second**

The speed of an object can be measured in miles
per hour or _____ per _____ . To find an object's
speed, you must find the _____ travelled and the
_____ taken. (Level 3)

2 What happens to the stopping distance as a car
moves faster? (Level 3)

3 Using the diagram below, what is the thinking
distance for a driver travelling at 30 mph? (Level
4)

4 Calculate the speed of a car that has travelled
100 miles in 2 hours. (Level 5)

5 How would the thinking distance and the braking
distance be affected if you were using a mobile
phone while driving? (Level 6)

5.6 Investigating falling objects

1 What did Aristotle think made some objects
fall faster than others? (Level 3)

2 What variables did Galileo keep the same when
doing his experiment? (Level 4)

3 Why is dropping objects with different weights
and shapes not a fair test? (Level 5)

4 Explain what would happen if a feather and a
hammer were dropped from the same height.
(Level 6)

Typical stopping distances ▼

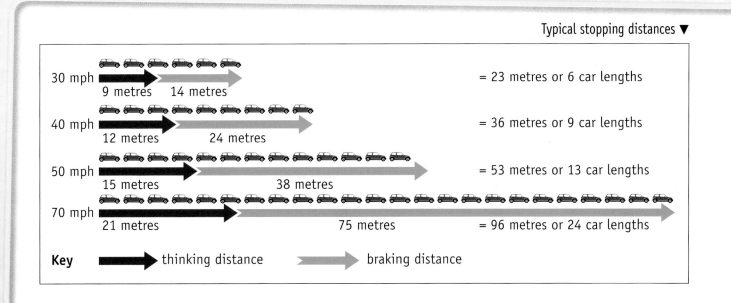

30 mph	9 metres 14 metres	= 23 metres or 6 car lengths
40 mph	12 metres 24 metres	= 36 metres or 9 car lengths
50 mph	15 metres 38 metres	= 53 metres or 13 car lengths
70 mph	21 metres 75 metres	= 96 metres or 24 car lengths

Key   ➤ thinking distance   ➤ braking distance

6.1 Wind and sunshine

There are lots of different sources of energy. Wind farms use special turbines to harness the power of the wind and generate electricity. The Sun is the major source of energy on the Earth. Plants that lived millions of years ago trapped the Sun's energy. We can use this trapped energy today.

- Make a list of some of the different types of energy you use every day.

- What is the major source of energy on the Earth?

- A fuel is something that can be burnt to release energy. List as many fuels as you can.

Coming up in this Chapter ...

6.2 Energy everywhere

Learn about:
- the different forms of energy
- how energy can be transferred

A rock concert ▲

Any object that has been bent, squashed or stretched has **strain energy**.

Energy that is stored in materials is called **chemical energy**.

Any object that can fall has **gravitational energy**.

There is a lot of energy at a concert, but what do we mean by energy? The word energy is used all the time, but in science it means something special. Energy makes things happen.

Types of energy

The band members are moving. Any moving object has movement energy or **kinetic energy**. The instruments make sounds. This is a type of energy called **sound energy**. No concert would be complete without a good light show. When an object gives out light, it gives out **light energy**. Concerts get very hot, and this too is a type of energy called heat energy or thermal energy. Amplifiers use electricity to make the guitars sound louder – they are using **electrical energy**.

A What types of energy are there at a concert? (Level 3)

Gas is a fuel and has ▶ chemical energy stored in it

▲ The diving board has been bent. It has strain energy. The diver has gravitational energy

128

Stored energy

Some objects have energy that is waiting to be used. We say they have stored energy or **potential energy**. There are different types of potential energy.

B What type of potential energy is stored in (i) a clockwork toy, (ii) a book on a shelf, (iii) a battery? (Level 4)

Transferring energy

Energy can be moved from place to place. Scientists call this an **energy transfer**. It is when energy is transferred that things happen. Look at the picture of the Bunsen burner. The energy comes into the Bunsen burner as chemical energy. It goes out as light energy and thermal energy.

Scientists use arrows to show energy transfers. The arrows show the type of energy coming in and going out. This is called an energy transfer diagram.

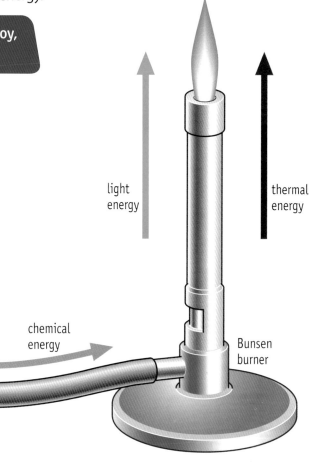

light energy

thermal energy

chemical energy

Bunsen burner

The Bunsen burner ▲

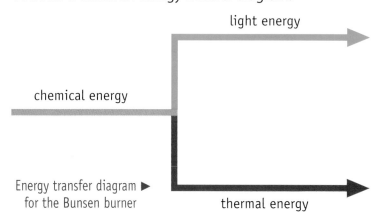

light energy

chemical energy

Energy transfer diagram ▶
for the Bunsen burner

thermal energy

C Draw an energy transfer diagram for a clockwork toy. (Level 5)

D What is the energy transfer in a bow and arrow? Draw an energy transfer diagram. (Level 6)

Science to the rescue

Red LEDs (light emitting diodes) give off red light but waste far less energy than a normal light bulb. If every traffic light in the country used them, we would save enough energy to close one power station.

Keywords
chemical energy, electrical energy, energy transfer, gravitational energy, kinetic energy, light energy, potential energy, sound energy, strain energy

6.3 Food, glorious food

Learn about:
- how much energy different people need
- how to compare the energy in food

A rugby player ... ▼

... and his food! ▶

Sportsmen and women need a lot of energy. Just like us, they get this energy from food.

To keep a healthy weight you need to understand how much energy you need and how much energy you get from food.

Energy in food

Food is our body's fuel. It is a store of chemical energy. We measure energy in **joules** (J). How many joules of energy you need depends on things such as your age, how active you are and how fast you are growing.

How much energy do you need?

Daily energy needs	
Person	Energy required per day (kJ)
Boy (12–15 years)	11 700
Girl (12–15 years)	9700
Rugby player	16 700
Manual worker	15 000
Male office worker	11 000
Female office worker	9800
Pregnant woman	10 000

Take a look at the table on the previous page showing the energy required by different people.

A How much energy do you need every day? (Level 3)

B Why do manual workers need more energy than office workers? (Level 4)

C Why does a 13-year-old boy need more energy than an office worker? (Level 5)

Finding the energy in food

You can find the energy in packaged food by reading the labels. Notice that the label tells you the amount of energy per packet and the amount of energy per 100 grams.

D When comparing the energy in food, why is looking at the energy per 100 g more useful than looking at the total energy? (Level 6)

Finding the energy by experimenting

If food is not in a packet, you can sometimes find the energy in the food by burning it. When food burns it releases chemical energy. If you burn food under a test tube containing water, the chemical energy in the food is transferred into heat energy and the water heats up. This is shown in the diagram below. The hotter the water gets, the more energy was in the food.

Food label ▼

	Per pack	Per 100g
ENERGY	630 kJ	2100 kJ
	150 kcal	500 kcal
PROTEIN	2 g	7 g
FAT	8 g	27 g
FIBRE	0.9 g	3 g
SODIUM	0.16 g	0.54 g
CARBOHYDRATE	18 g	60 g

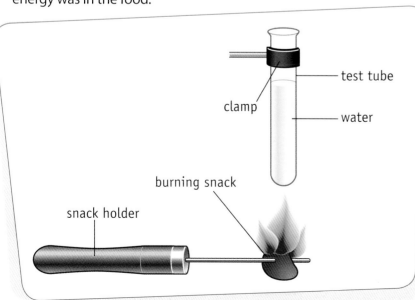

test tube

clamp

water

burning snack

snack holder

Keyword
joule

6.4 Our friend the Sun

Learn about:
- how the Earth gets most of its energy
- energy sources provided by the Sun
- which sources of energy are suitable for the UK

Most people enjoy a sunny day by the sea, but the Sun does more than keep us warm and let us see things – in fact nearly all the Earth's energy comes originally from the Sun. The world is running out of energy resources such as oil, coal and gas. Energy from the Sun can be used to replace these resources.

A day at the seaside ▲

◀ A solar power station in France ▼

Energy from the Sun

Energy from the Sun is sometimes called **solar energy**.

> **A** What two types of energy can you detect from the Sun? (Level 3)

There are many ways we can use the energy from the Sun. Heat from the Sun makes the wind, which blows on the sails of **wind turbines**. As they turn, the wind's energy is transfered into electrical energy. The Sun also makes waves, which can turn **wave turbines**. These transfer the kinetic energy of the waves into electrical energy. Light from the Sun can be used directly to make electricity from **solar cells**, which can be put on the roofs of houses.

Getting energy from the Sun ▼

1

heat energy from the Sun

causes the air to rise as it gets warmer

a calm sea

2

colder air blows in to replace the warm air, gaining kinetic energy as it moves faster

the wind blows on the ocean, making waves

3

the wind makes the wind turbine turn

the waves make the wave turbine turn

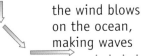

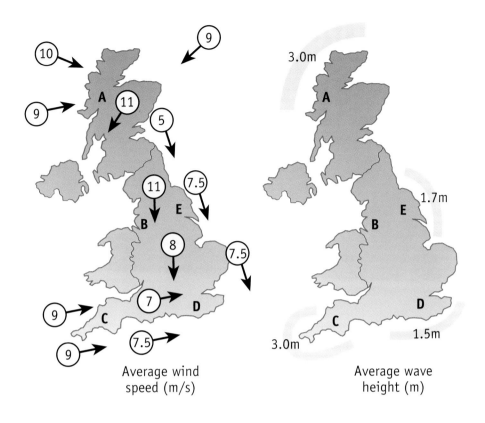

Average wind speed (m/s)

Average wave height (m)

Average hours of sunlight per day

▲ Average wind speeds, wave heights and sunlight hours in the UK

Renewable energy

As the Sun shines every day, wind, wave and solar energy are called **renewable energy** sources. This means they will never run out, unlike oil, coal and gas which are examples of **non-renewable energy** sources – one day they will be used up. Making electricity from the Sun's energy also causes no air pollution.

B What are the advantages of using the Sun's energy to make electricity, compared with using fossil fuels such as oil, coal and gas? (Level 4)

Britain and Ireland have a temperate climate – it does not get very hot or very cold – but we do get a lot of wind and rough seas.

C Places A, B, C, D and E are shown on the maps above. Where would you build a wind turbine and a wave turbine? Explain your decisions. (Level 5)

D Where do you think is the most suitable place in the UK to have a solar cell on your roof? Explain why. (Level 6)

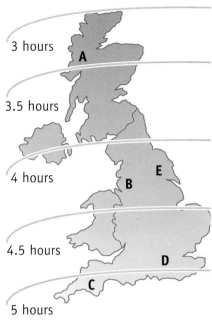

Science to the rescue

King Island, near Australia, gets all its electricity from a rechargeable battery. Wind turbines charge up a massive battery when the wind blows, and all the islanders' houses are connected to it.

Keywords
non-renewable energy, renewable energy, solar cell, solar energy, wave turbine, wind turbine

6.5 Time detectives

All of Britain was like this once! ▲

Under the ground in many parts of the UK are large amounts of **coal**. The coal was formed from the remains of dead plants that grew in hot swampy conditions. This means that the UK must have once been hot and swampy.

Oil and **natural gas** are also found in rocks deep underground. They are made from the remains of dead animals. A fossil is an impression of a dead plant or animal preserved in rock or coal, so scientists call these fuels **fossil fuels**.

A What are coal, oil and natural gas called? (Level 3)

How coal was formed ▼

Plants trapped the energy in sunlight

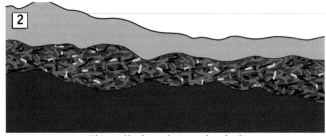
They died and were buried

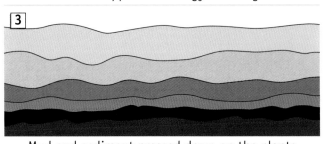
Mud and sediment pressed down on the plants

This turned the mud into rock and the plants into coal

The UK's coal and oil

There is coal underground in the UK and oil under the seas around its coast. But the UK is not hot and swampy, so why do we have these resources? To find out, we must go back in time…

300 million years ago

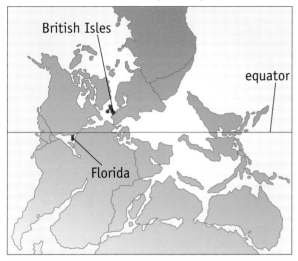

Today

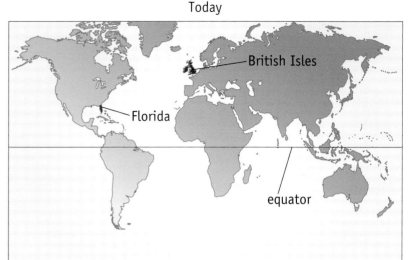

How the Earth has changed ▲

Most coal was formed from plants that grew 300 million years ago. You can see from the first map that the UK was near the equator all those years ago, so conditions then were very different. The second map shows where the UK is now.

B Why was the UK a hotter place 300 million years ago? (Level 4)

C Florida, in the USA, has a lot of swampy forests and is much nearer the equator than the UK is today, more like the UK was 300 million years ago. What might be happening to the dead trees in Florida's swamps? (Level 5)

Why fossil fuels are important

We are lucky to have fossil fuels in the UK because a lot of energy is stored in them. We can burn them to release thermal energy. This can be used to produce steam. Steam can be used to power machinery and to generate electricity in power stations.

D Why can we not be certain when fossil fuels will run out? (Level 6)

Fossil fuels are eventually going to run out. They are non-renewable. This means they are not being replaced as we use them up. Scientists all over the world are working together to try to find alternative sources of energy to fossil fuels.

Foul fact

Peat is a type of unfinished coal. Sometimes bodies of people are found in peat bogs, with their skin turned into leather.

Keywords
coal, fossil fuel, natural gas, oil

6.6 Why conserve fuels?

Learn about:
- different types of fuel
- conserving fuels

◀ Burning animal dung

Would you like to use dung to cook with? Think of the smell and where it comes from. Today we have different fuels to choose from. We're running out of some types of fuels and must do our best to conserve them. We also have newer versions of the fuel in the photo, which may play a part in providing energy in the future.

Fossil fuels

We have already seen that fossil fuels are non-renewable. This means that one day they will run out.

The chart shows how long the different fossil fuels are expected to last. The dates are called estimates, which means scientists cannot be sure about them. One reason is that we might save much more energy, which would make fossil fuels last longer. We need other sources of energy to replace fossil fuels when they run out.

Predicted dates when we will run out of fossil fuels ▼

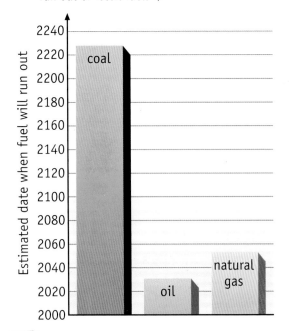

A Which fossil fuel is expected to run out first? (Level 3)

B According to the estimates, how many years will it be before we use up all the coal, oil and natural gas? (Level 4)

What are the alternatives?

One alternative to fossil fuels is a **nuclear** fuel called **uranium**. This is also mined from under the ground.

- Uranium breaks down naturally to produce a lot of thermal energy, which is much more concentrated than the energy in fossil fuels.
- Unlike burning fossil fuels, the breakdown of uranium does not cause pollution.
- But it is hard to control and makes very dangerous waste products that are very expensive to get rid of.

We can also use animal and plant material, such as sugar, as fuel. These materials are called **biomass** and can also be used to make electricity.

As plants grow, they absorb carbon dioxide from the air. When they are burnt, they release the same amount of carbon dioxide back again, so they don't cause any extra pollution. But they contain less energy than fossil fuels. Biomass is a type of renewable energy

▲ Demonstrating against nuclear power

C Think about nuclear fuel and biomass. Write down one advantage and one disadvantage of each compared to fossil fuels. (Level 5)

▲ The Citroen C1 can do 83 mpg

Why conserving energy is important

The world has enough oil for about 25 years and enough uranium for about 60 years. After this we could run out of energy supplies, so we must conserve as much energy as possible.

New cars are being developed that use less petrol, and more efficient power stations are being designed. You can help in small ways too by turning off lights at home and turning off the TV instead of using standby buttons.

Interesting fact

In Brazil, over half the new cars sold run on fuel made from sugar. The sugar is turned into a type of alcohol, which can be used in car engines, just like petrol.

D How do you think cars are designed to use less petrol? (Level 6)

Keywords
biomass, nuclear, uranium

6.7 Heating up the Earth

D

Learn about:
- how humans have changed the Earth's atmosphere
- what the greenhouse effect is
- how changes to the Earth's atmosphere can be studied

How the greenhouse effect works ▼

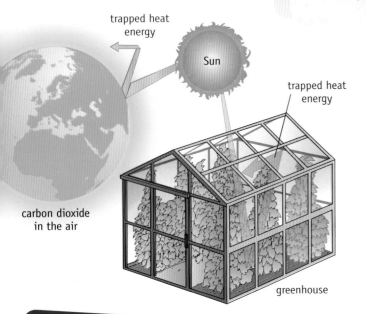

trapped heat energy

Sun

trapped heat energy

carbon dioxide in the air

greenhouse

▲ Driving cars affects the Earth's atmosphere

Burning fuels such as coal, oil and gas give us light energy and heat energy, and make things move. But it also releases carbon dioxide into the Earth's **atmosphere**. The atmosphere is the layer of air that surrounds the Earth. Most scientists think that we are changing it, which could cause huge problems.

The greenhouse effect

In a greenhouse, the glass stops some of the heat energy from escaping. This keeps the plants warm. The carbon dioxide in the atmosphere has the same effect on the Earth as the glass in a greenhouse.

The Sun's energy heats up the Earth. Carbon dioxide in the atmosphere stops some of the heat energy escaping from the Earth. This keeps the Earth warm. This is called the **greenhouse effect**, and carbon dioxide is called a **greenhouse gas**. You can see how this works in the diagram.

A   Why is carbon dioxide called a greenhouse gas? (Level 3)

Relationships

Most scientists agree that there is a **relationship** between the temperature of the Earth and the amount of carbon dioxide in the atmosphere. As the level of carbon dioxide rises, the Earth gets hotter.

Scientists at work

The millions of cows around the world produce a lot of methane, by burping and farting. Methane is another gas which causes the Earth to warm up. Kangaroos do not produce methane because it is used up by a special type of bacteria in their stomachs. Scientists want to try to put these bacteria inside cows to reduce the greenhouse effect.

Ryan and Amber decide to do an experiment to find out about the relationship between the temperature of the Earth and the amount of carbon dioxide in the atmosphere. It is difficult to measure big changes to the Earth, so they design a model to represent the Earth. The model uses a **biodome**, a much smaller version of the ones at the Eden Project in Cornwall.

Carbon dioxide is added through the tube at the side. The carbon dioxide level and the temperature inside the dome are recorded by a computer. An **input** or **independent variable** is a **variable** that you change in an experiment. An **output** or **dependent variable** is the variable that changes and is measured.

> **B** What are the input and output variables in the biodome experiment? (Level 4)

The biodome experiment

Ryan and Amber run the experiment for five days. Each day they increase the level of carbon dioxide to see if there is a relationship between carbon dioxide level and temperature. Scientists use the word 'relationship' to describe how the output variable changes when the input variable is changed. At the end of five days, Ryan and Amber create a graph on the computer with their results. The graph of temperature against carbon dioxide level shows the relationship.

The biodome experiment ▼

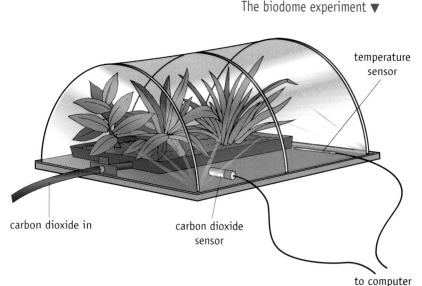

carbon dioxide in

carbon dioxide sensor

temperature sensor

to computer

Results of the biodome experiment ▼

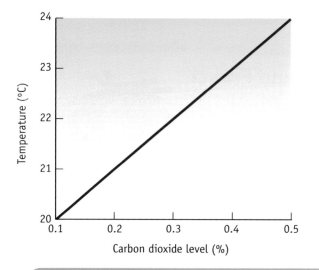

> **C** Explain what the graph shows about the relationship between carbon dioxide level and temperature. (Level 5)

> **D** Scientists use models to predict future changes to the Earth. Use the results from the biodome experiment to predict what you think will happen to the temperature of the Earth over the next 10 years. (Level 6)

Keywords
atmosphere, biodome, dependent variable, greenhouse effect, greenhouse gas, independent variable, input variable, output variable, relationship, variable

6.8 Different countries, different solutions

Learn about:
- why different countries generate electricity in different ways

A nuclear power station in France ▲

Science to the rescue

Scientists are developing more efficient renewable energies all the time, reducing our need for fossil fuels and nuclear fuels.

Different countries in Europe generate electricity in different ways. This is because different countries have different resources and cultures. France produces more electricity using nuclear power than any other country in Europe. They continue to build new nuclear power stations, while Germany has passed a law called the Nuclear Exit Law that means its nuclear power stations must close by 2020.

Comparing the UK and France

In the UK, about 20% of our electricity is made using nuclear fuel. In France it is over 70%.

Britain and France are separated by a thin strip of water, so why is there a big difference? Let's look at how much fossil fuel each country has.

Energy data for the UK and France (2003)	Millions of tonnes	
	UK	France
Coal production	31	2
Gas production	4	0.1
Oil production	2393	76
Consumption of energy	1794	2083

A Which country produces the most coal, gas and oil? (Level 3)

B Calculate the difference between energy consumption and production for both countries. (Level 4)

C Why do you think France uses much more nuclear fuel than Britain? (Level 5)

England ▼

Electricity from water

Another way of producing energy is by using falling water in a hydroelectric power station. Water falls from a reservoir and turns a turbine to produce electricity. This type of energy requires the right kind of environment.

China has built the largest hydroelectric power station in the world. It cost around £25 billion. The lake behind the dam flooded so much land that 1.3 million people had to find new homes.

D Look at the photos of England and Norway. Which country do you think produces the most electricity from falling water? Explain your answer. (Level 6)

Norway ▲

We have brought in the Nuclear Exit law because we feel nuclear power is unsafe.

Why Germany said no to nuclear

So why has Germany decided that its nuclear power stations must close by 2020? In Germany there is a large Green Party which is part of the government. This party believes that it is very important to look after the environment.

141

9 The personal robot

Will you ever have a personal robot – to tidy your room, find your shoes and do your homework? Would you like to have a personal music system that fits into a set of headphones and plays you the right tune before you even ask ... by reading your mind?

These inventions will almost certainly be powered by electricity. Electricity has already given us electronic games and robotic mice.

- Draw a circuit with a lamp, switch and cell.

- Imagine you have your own personal robot. How does it move – on legs or wheels? How is it powered?

- Make a list of things that use electricity. Then split your list into two parts: one list of things that plug in and one of things that use batteries.

Coming up in this Chapter ...

6.10 Robots and phones

Learn about:
- why batteries don't last for ever
- why portable gadgets are designed to be as energy-efficient as possible

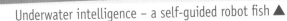

Underwater intelligence – a self-guided robot fish ▲

Interesting fact

Scientists have discovered a way to convert the energy in sugar into electricity. They say that one day people could recharge their phones by refilling the cells with tree sap or a squirt of a soft drink.

A robot fish swims beside an oil pipeline, looking for leaks. Suddenly its sensors indicate that its battery is running low. At once it begins to search the sea bed. It knows there is a recharging station down there somewhere. Ah yes – found it. A shark swims by and the robot takes its photo before getting on with job of recharging. It's just another typical moment in the life of a robot fish.

How the robot swims

The robot fish swims like a real fish by swaying its tail and body. It gets the energy to move from its batteries or **cells**. Cells are stores of energy. Each cell converts stored chemical energy into electrical energy. Cells contain materials that react and release energy. These materials take up space, which is why it is difficult to make a really small battery.

Making the robot fish move uses a lot of energy and drains the cells quickly. If it 'rests', the fish can sense its surroundings for days without recharging. But resting is not an option for a robot with a job to do, so the inventors are looking for other ways to make the cells last longer.

> **A** Why can the robot fish keep going longer if it doesn't move? (Level 3)

The tooth phone

The mobile phone in the photo is so small that it can be strapped to your tooth. So when will this marvellous phone be for sale? Right now it is still in the lab because there isn't a tiny cell that can supply it with electricity.

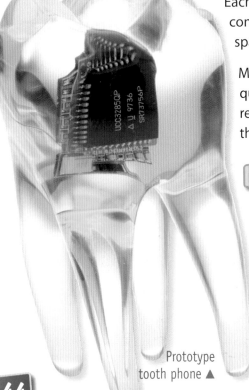

Prototype tooth phone ▲

> **B** The tooth phone doesn't need to have any lights or even a loudspeaker. How does this affect its electrical energy needs, and why? (Level 4)

Why size matters

In mobile devices, engineers want the cells to be as small as possible to reduce the weight. The problem is that a small cell doesn't hold much stored energy. The robot in the photo below must recharge its cells every half-hour.

C A tiny 'button cell' keeps a digital watch running for months. What does this tell you about the amount of energy that a watch needs? (Level 5)

Cells come in all shapes and sizes ▲

The drive for small and light

The cells in early mobile phones were as heavy as a bag of sugar. These phones needed a lot of energy to work. Modern mobile phones use energy more efficiently and have smaller, lighter cells. More portable devices are appearing all the time. Perhaps you already have a portable music player or computer. The next step will surely be your dream personal cell-powered robot.

Scientists at work

There are robot mice, robotic cows, robots in sewers, robots on Mars, robots that hop, fly and swim. Advances in robotics happen daily. But with every triumph, there are a lot more challenges waiting for a scientist to solve.

D Currently Asimo's batteries have to be recharged every half-hour. Why did the scientists not give the robot larger cells? (Level 6)

ASIMO

HONDA

▲ Asimo – a humanoid, personal robot takes a break to recharge its cells

Early mobile phones were often called 'bricks' ▼

Keyword
cell

145

6.11 Blowing a fuse

Learn about:
- how traditional light bulbs produce light
- how a fuse protects the other components in a circuit
- how models can help illustrate what happens with current

Laser show ▲

The tungsten wire in a bulb ▼

There are many devices that produce light – from candles to lasers. Light is energy, and the energy has to come from somewhere. In the case of a light bulb, energy is transferred to the bulb by the electric **current**.

How it works

Traditional light bulbs have a thin wire made of tungsten. This heats up when current flows through it. It glows white-hot. But this way of producing light is wasteful because a lot of the electrical energy is converted to heat rather than light. There are more energy-efficient ways to make light.

 A | What two forms of energy do traditional light bulbs give out? (Level 3)

Interesting fact

Street lamps produce light more efficiently than traditional bulbs, but they give out only yellow light. This is why they're used to light streets and not homes.

Blowing a fuse

Nina, an engineer with a space agency, puts on her safety glasses and shows her team how a **fuse** works. She sets up a circuit with three cells and a few thin wires of steel wool held between crocodile clips. The steel wool is resting on a heat resistant mat. There is an **ammeter** to measure current.

This light is made of LEDs which are ▶ tiny energy-efficient light sources

The switch is closed and current flows. The steel wires glow red-hot. Nina adds another cell and closes the switch. This time, the steel wires sparkle and burn out. The reading on the ammeter drops to zero.

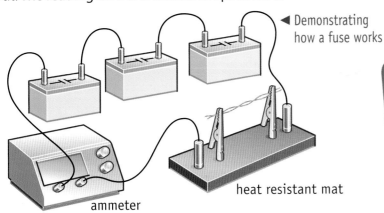

◀ Demonstrating how a fuse works

ammeter

heat resistant mat

B When the ammeter reading drops to zero, what has happened to the current? (Level 4)

This is how an electric fuse works. If there is a surge of current, the fuse wire in the fuse heats up and melts, breaking the circuit.

C When and how does a fuse break a circuit? (Level 5)

An explosion in space

Fuses can prevent disasters like the one that almost killed the crew of Apollo 13. The trouble began when the insulation around two wires was damaged during pre-flight testing. Not long after take-off, the wires touched, and the short-circuit heated the wires up and caused a fire. Soon after, an oxygen tank exploded. The astronauts made it safely back to Earth but it was a close call. A fuse would probably have prevented this ordeal.

Models of electricity

One way to imagine a current is to think of a huge circle of people walking around a circuit, each holding five cotton-wool balls. The balls represent packets of energy. As the people walk through components such as light bulbs or buzzers, they hand over a packet or two of energy. When the people pass through the cell, they pick up a fresh handful of cotton-wool balls.

Scientists use models to visualise their ideas but models are never perfect. Other models for current include water flowing in pipes (see the picture on the right) and even blood in the body.

Apollo 13 ▲

The water model of electricity ▼

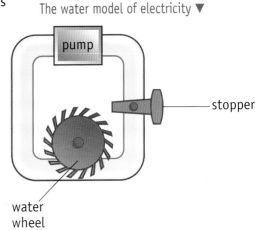

pump

stopper

water wheel

Keywords
ammeter, current, fuse

D In the water model of a circuit, what might a pump represent? (Level 6)

6.12 Circuits

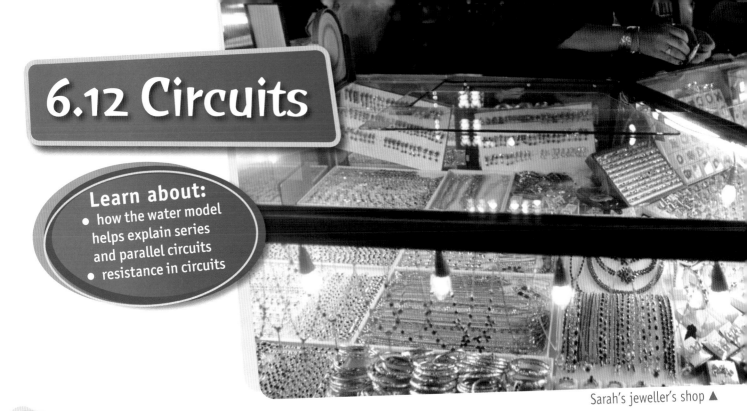

Learn about:
- how the water model helps explain series and parallel circuits
- resistance in circuits

Sarah's jeweller's shop ▲

Interesting fact

The hazard lights in a car are used together. But the bulbs are usually wired in parallel, so if one bulb fails or is hit during an accident, the other lights still flash.

Sarah manages a jeweller's shop. One morning she switches on the spotlights inside the jewellery display cabinets. But in one cabinet, only one of the two spotlights comes on. Sarah is puzzled. She knows that electricity flows in a circuit. Now that one bulb has blown, surely the circuit is broken. Why is one bulb still lit?

Series and parallel

Sarah imagined that the bulbs were in a **series circuit.** A series circuit is one in which there is only one path for the current to flow. It goes through all the bulbs in turn.

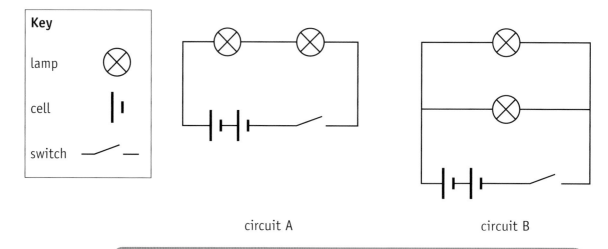

circuit A   circuit B

A Which circuit, A or B, has only one path for the current? (Level 3)

The answer is that the bulbs are in a **parallel circuit**. The wire from the cell splits into two branches that later join up again. If one bulb is blown, current still flows to the other bulb and back to the cell, so this bulb stays lit.

B | Which of the circuits, A or B, is a parallel circuit? Explain why. (Level 4)

An electronic game

In Ryan's electronic game, you move the metal ring along the wriggly wire as smoothly as possible. If the ring touches the wire, the buzzer buzzes and the bulb lights up.

Jasmine says the buzzer does the same job as the bulb. Ryan takes it out and touches the ring on the wire. 'That's odd. The bulb looks brighter now,' says Ryan. 'Why?'

'Maybe there's less **resistance** now,' says Jasmine.

In the water model of electricity (see page 147), resistance is like an obstacle inside the water pipe, slowing the flow. All components have some resistance. Without the buzzer, there's less resistance.

Ryan's game ▲

C | Reducing the resistance in the circuit changes the current. Use the water model to predict how it changes. (Level 5)

'We have removed some resistance so there's more current. Current carries energy. So the bulb is brighter because it's getting more energy,' says Ryan.

A buzz game with a parallel circuit

Amber's game is better because there's a lamp to show if the game is ready to play. The lamp and buzzer are in parallel. This means the lamp stays bright even when the buzzer sounds.

D | If Amber replaces the buzzer with a louder one, will this change the brightness of the bulb? Why or why not? (Level 6)

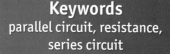

Keywords
parallel circuit, resistance, series circuit

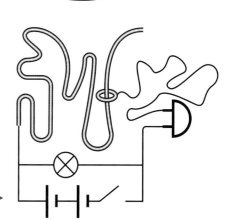

How Amber's game works ▶

6.13 Lightning strike

Learn about:
- killer currents
- how science explains the mystery of a lightning strike

This tree was set alight by lightning ▲

A flash of light tears across the sky and sets a tree on fire or leaves a victim dead – it is no wonder that long ago people thought that lightning came from angry gods. Can science help explain what happens when lightning strikes? The article below describes what can happen.

Teacher struck by lightning

Charlie Sutton admitted, 'I should be dead.' The 24-year-old teacher was struck on the back of the head by a lightning bolt as he guided pupils across a bridge. He said, 'It was like being hit with 100 baseball bats all at once. Someone said they saw this fork of lightning strike my head and I just fell to the ground.

'At the hospital the doctors were amazed. They said it was a miracle I was alive. I had an entry burn but the doctors couldn't work out where the electric charge had left my body. I was incredibly lucky.'

So what is an entry burn? Why was Charlie hit rather than his pupils? Was he really lucky to survive?

Interesting fact

The chances of being struck by lightning are about one in three million.

The strength of a lightning bolt

The number of volts of an electrical supply tells you its strength. The D-type cell in the photo gives 1.5 volts (or 1.5 V). The electrical supply in your home is about 230 volts. A lightning strike might have a strength of 300,000 volts. This suggests that it would kill its victim every time, but in fact four out of five people survive. Why?

A Two D-type cells placed in series produce a voltage of 3 V (1.5 V + 1.5 V). How could you produce a voltage of 6 V using D-type cells? (Level 3)

A 'killer' electric shock

It is not actually the voltage of a lightning strike that causes harm – it is the current it produces. If an electric current flows through a person, it can stop their heart from beating. It can also cause burns. Skin is a poor conductor, meaning that electrical energy is changed to heat energy as the current passes through it. This is why electric shock victims suffer 'entry and exit burns'.

In the case of lightning, the current stops flowing after just a few milliseconds. Victims may be burnt and suffer a heart attack but they often survive if medical help comes quickly.

> **B** Why do lightning victims often survive? (Level 4)

Staying safe

Scientific knowledge can help people stay safe. Some metals, such as copper, are very good conductors. Metal rods called lightning conductors are fitted to church spires and other tall buildings. The lightning flows to the ground through the metal rather than the wet brick or stone of the building.

Lightning takes the easiest route to the ground, and air is a poor conductor. So if you are in a lightning storm, stay away from trees and keep low, so that the lightning doesn't take the option of flowing through you!

Lightning victims sometimes say their clothes were blown off. An electric current always flows along the easiest path. Dry skin is not a good conductor but water is a very good conductor. If the person's clothes are wet from rain, most of the current takes this path. This rapidly heats up the water in the clothes, produces a burst of steam and blows the clothes off.

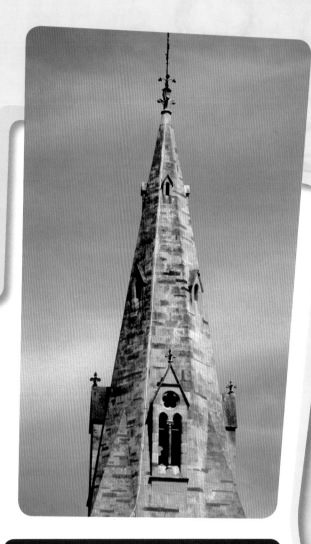

> **C** How does the lightning conductor on a church spire work? (Level 5)

> **D** Why should you squat down if you are caught in a lightning storm? (Level 6)

You should never mess with electricity. A shock from the mains electricity supply in your home can kill. At 230 volts, the mains produces enough current to paralyse the muscles, so you may be trapped gripping a live wire.

What's next?

Science can explain many of the effects of a lightning strike, though some mysteries remain. But no one has found a way to harness this powerful source of energy.

6.14 ELECTRICITY FROM THE HUMBLE SPUD!

Written by Jonathan Hare, co-presenter of BBC's Rough Science series

Best Science Lesson Ever

Learn about

- how to make your own electrical cell
- how to connect cells to make series and parallel circuits

Electricity from potatoes! ▼

Without electrical cells, our radios, mp3 players, mobile phones and a thousand other things wouldn't work. We are going to find out how to make cells with the help of a few potatoes.

What is a cell?

A cell converts chemical energy into electricity. A carbon rod, a zinc-plated screw and the chemicals in a potato are enough to make a simple cell.

A   How does a cell make electricity? (Level 3)

Before you start

You can make cells from lemons, oranges, or even a cup of sea (salt) water, but potatoes are less messy.

You will need to get into groups of five. Make sure you have a pad of paper, the equipment you will need, and a clear and clean table top.

Each group will need:
- 6 potatoes
- 6 zinc-plated screws
- 6 carbon rods
- 15 crocodile-clip leads
- an LED light
- a voltmeter
- a buzzer

Make your own cell

Push two carbon rods into a potato. Measure the **voltage** between them by connecting the voltmeter to the two rods. Note down the voltage. Now try two screws instead. What is the voltage now?

Now try using one screw and one carbon rod. What does the meter read now? Can you get the LED or the buzzer to work by connecting it to the potato cell?

B Which type of potato cell works best: with two carbon rods, with two screws, or with one screw and one rod? (Level 4)

Three potato cells ▼

carbon rod   zinc-plated screw

+   −

potato

Foul fact

If you have a brace on your teeth, your saliva and the foil from a sweet wrapper can form a cell. It tastes horrible and it tingles because it's slightly electrocuting you!

More electricity please

There is very little electricity from one spud cell. You need to wire a few cells together to do anything useful. Cells joined together are called a **battery**. We can use a series or a parallel circuit of cells for a battery.

To get more voltage, you wire the cells in series. In a series circuit only the beginning screw and end rod become our battery connections. The rod on each potato is connected to the screw on the next potato, and so on. Wire two potato cells in series and measure the voltage at the ends. Try three, four, five and six potato cells in series and note the voltages.

Wiring cells in parallel will add the currents together. Every rod is wired to another rod and every screw is wired to another screw. The wiring is quite different from the series circuit. Now try out these two types of circuit to power the LED and then the buzzer.

+ −

Potato cells in series ▲
Potato cells in parallel ▼

− +

C The LED light needs as much voltage as possible, while the buzzer needs as much current as possible. Which circuits (series or parallel) would work best for the LED and buzzer? (Level 5)

The super-spud battery

Each group should bring a six-potato series battery to a clear table and wire them all in parallel to make a super-spud battery. Can you get enough electricity to operate a small radio or TV remote control?

group 1 battery

group 2 battery

group 3 battery

+   A super-spud battery ▲   −   add more ...

Keywords
battery, voltage

153

6 Assess your progress

6.2 Energy everywhere

1 What is another name for heat energy? (Level 3)

2 Copy and complete the sentences using these words: **transferred energy kinetic potential**
_____ is needed to make things happen. An object that is moving has _____ energy. If an object has energy waiting to be used, it has _____ energy. For something to happen, energy is _____ from one place to another. (Level 3)

3 Which has more potential energy: a ball on a table, or a ball on the floor? (Level 4)

4 What type of potential energy do the following objects have? **a** a hot air balloon; **b** a firework; **c** a squashed ball. (Level 5)

5 Draw an energy transfer diagram for a bonfire burning. (Level 6)

6.3 Food, glorious food

1 What unit do we measure energy in? (Level 3)

2 Copy and complete the sentences using these words: **chemical food the Sun**
We get our energy from _____. Energy is stored in it as _____ energy. The energy in our food comes from _____. (Level 3)

3 What affects how much energy a person needs every day? (Level 4)

4 Why do you think an average male office worker needs more energy than an average female office worker? (Level 5)

5 Why do you need more energy in the winter than in the summer? (Level 6)

6.4 Our friend the Sun

1 What do both wind energy and wave energy have in common? (Level 3)

2 Copy and complete the sentences using these words: **light renewable temperature heat solar**
Energy from the Sun is called _____ energy. Wind and waves are caused by _____ from the Sun making the air move. _____ from the Sun can be used to power calculators (Level 3)

3 Why do you think that in the UK there are lots of wind turbines being built, but not many solar cells? (Level 4)

4 If you had a solar cell on your roof, how would the amount of energy you received from it change throughout the day? (Level 5)

5 Sudan is a country in Central Africa. How would the methods used to generate electricity from the Sun differ from those used in the UK? (Level 6)

6.5 Time detectives

1 If new coal is being made today, why do we call it a non-renewable fuel? (Level 3)

2 Copy and complete the sentences using these words: **millions animals fossil plants non-renewable**
Coal, oil and natural gas are called _____ fuels. They were formed from _____ and _____ that lived _____ of years ago. Fossil fuels will run out, so we call them _____. (Level 3)

3 How do we know that fossil fuels are not being formed around the UK today? (Level 4)

4 What conditions do you think cause plant and animal remains to change into fossil fuels when they are deep underground? (Level 5)

5 Most of the Earth's coal was produced during a period in history called the carboniferous period. How do you think the Earth was different then from how it is today? (Level 6)

6.6 Why conserve fuels?

1 Name a nuclear fuel. (Level 3).

2 Copy and complete the sentences using these words: **energy   concentrated   pollution   non-renewable**

We produce a lot of our energy from fossil fuels because the energy is _____. This means you get a lot of _____ from them. The disadvantages of using them are that they are _____ and they cause _____ . (Level 3)

3 Which fuels do not add to pollution in the atmosphere? (Level 4)

4 Why are trees a renewable energy source? (Level 5)

5 The Earth only has enough coal reserves to last another 230 years, so what is the problem with using just coal to provide us with energy? (Level 6)

6.7 Heating up the Earth

1 Which fuels, when burned, add to the greenhouse effect? (Level 3)

2 Name two greenhouse gases. (Level 3)

3 What happens in a greehouse to cause it to warm up? (Level 4)

4 What do you think the temperature in Ryan and Amber's biodome on page 139 will be when the carbon dioxide level is 1.0%? (Level 5)

5 Do you think that there is a relationship between carbon dioxide level and the temperature of the Earth? Expalin your answer. (Level 6)

6.8 Different countries, different solutions

1 Copy and complete the sentences using these words: **20%   France   hydroelectric**

_____ produces around 70% of its energy from nuclear power stations. In Britain it is around _____ . Norway produces a lot of its electricity using _____ power. (Level 3)

2 How do hydroelectric power stations produce electricity? (Level 4)

3 If Germany shuts down its nuclear plants, in what other ways could it produce electricity? (Level 5)

4 Is energy from falling water renewable or non-renewable? Explain your answer. (Level 6)

6.10 Robots and phones

1 What energy conversion happens in a cell? (Level 3)

2 A small AA cell and a larger D cell both give 1.5 volts. Which one has more energy? (Level 3)

3 Noah makes about 10 calls a day on his mobile phone, while Imogen uses hers only in an emergency. Whose phone cell lasts longer and why? (Level 4)

4 There is a new laptop which lasts for a month without recharging. It is heavier than a large suitcase. How has this extra cell-life been achieved? (Level 5)

5 Brainstorm a list of advantages, disadvantages and questions that you have regarding the tooth phone described on page 144. Is it a good thing? Why or why not? (Level 6)

6.11 Blowing a fuse

1 A light bulb in a simple circuit 'blows' and goes out. Is current now flowing in the circuit? (Level 3)

2 There are 1,000 milliamps in an amp. How many milliamps are there in 2 amps? (Level 3)

3 The switch on a simple circuit including an ammeter is opened. What does the reading on the ammeter say now? (Level 4)

4 In the blood model of current, what organ in the body could represent the battery? (Level 5)

5 Why are traditional light bulbs said to be wasteful? (Level 6)

Chapter 6 questions continued on page 169

The first amazing thing about space is how big it is. The nearest star to the Earth beyond our Sun is 40,000,000,000,000 km away. Even light takes four years to travel this distance.

The next amazing thing about space is how empty it is. We can only see the light from the nearest star, called Proxima Centauri, because there is almost nothing in the way to block it.

The third amazing thing about space is that it's there at all. Scientists calculate that the chance of a universe like ours existing – with galaxies, stars, planets and life – is almost zero.

- The planets in our Solar System are Mercury, Venus, Earth, Mars, Jupiter, Saturn, Uranus and Neptune. Which of the planets is closest to the Sun?

- Which planet rotates once every 24 hours and is thought to be the only planet in the Solar System with liquid water?

- What is the nearest star to the Earth, apart from the Sun?

Coming up in this Chapter ...

7.2 In a spin

Learn about:
- some different ways people have explained day and night
- how evidence supports the idea that the Earth rotates on its axis

The Earth seen from space ▲

If you photograph the stars every few minutes, you can see how they seem to move across the sky as the Earth rotates ▼

Long ago, people had very different ideas about how space works. They saw the Sun moving across the sky during the daytime. At night, they saw the **stars** rising and setting. We now know that we see this apparent movement of everything in space because the Earth **rotates** on its **axis**. But ancient people saw it as evidence that everything in Space moves around the Earth.

A | Why do people on Earth experience daytime and night-time? (Level 3)

B | How did people in the past explain daytime and night-time? (Level 4)

Evidence that doesn't fit

Four hundred years ago, the astronomer Galileo watched the **planets** with his telescope, which was then a recent invention. He saw moons orbiting around Jupiter. It got him wondering – perhaps everything in space does not go around the Earth …

◄ Through his telescope, Galileo saw things that no-one had seen before

The view from space

Shortly after the Second World War, scientists launched a camera into Space on a missile. Later, astronauts orbited the Earth and even saw the Earth from the Moon.

Their videos and pictures proved that the reason everything seems to go around us is that the Earth rotates. Each rotation takes one day, which is 24 hours. During half a day, one side of the Earth moves into darkness while the other side moves into daylight.

C **Explain how the Earth's rotation makes it look as if the Sun rises, moves across the sky and sets. (Level 5)**

D Night begins in France before it begins in Britain. On a globe, France is to the left of Britian. Does the Earth rotate clockwise or anticlockwise? (Level 6)

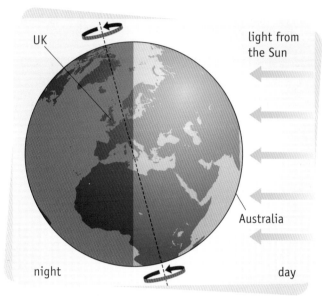

▲ Day and night

I can see why the Sun seems to move across the sky. If you spin on the spot, everything around you seems to move. But it's not the Sun that's moving – we are!

Eclipses

As well as rotating on its axis, the Earth also orbits round the Sun. It takes the Earth 365 days to orbit the Sun once. The Moon orbits round the Earth, taking 28 days. Sometimes the Moon and the Earth are lined up so that the Moon stops the Sun's light from reaching part of the Earth. This is called a **solar eclipse**. It is an eerie experience when the sky becomes dark even though it is daytime. At other times, the Moon moves into the Earth's shadow. This is called a **lunar eclipse** and the Moon looks reddish-brown.

solar eclipse (not to scale)

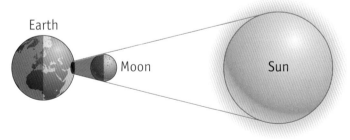

lunar eclipse (not to scale)

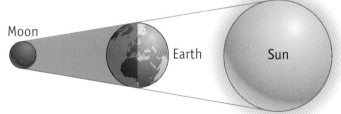

Keywords
axis, lunar eclipse, planet, rotate, solar eclipse, star

7.3 All about the Moon

Did US astronaut Buzz Aldrin really land on the Moon? ▲

Learn about:
- the controversy about whether humans landed on the Moon
- why the Moon seems to disappear and reappear each month

The Moon ▼

In 1969, Neil Armstrong and Buzz Aldrin became the first people to step onto the Moon. But there are a few people who claim that the American Space Agency, NASA, filmed the landing on the Moon in a movie studio on Earth! Scientists have proved that this is a ridiculous idea. Here's some of the evidence and scientific knowledge they use to prove their case.

The Moon's landscape

From Earth, the Moon looks white. But in the photo of Buzz Aldrin, the landscape looks grey. Does this mean that the photo might not have been taken on the Moon?

A Explain why we see the Moon as white. (Level 3)

Interesting fact

Some religious festivals are held when the Moon is in a particular phase. The Muslim festival of Eid ul Fitr is celebrated at the end of the month of Ramadan. The festival begins when the New Moon is first seen in the sky.

The Moon produces no light of its own. We see the Moon because light from the Sun bounces off the Moon and then reaches the Earth. In our dark night sky, the reflected light coming from the Moon makes it look silvery and bright. When you are actually on the Moon, the landscape looks grey, so the photo is correct.

Where are the stars?

In the photo of Buzz Aldrin there are no stars in the black sky. People who think that the astronauts didn't land on the Moon say that this is evidence that the photo wasn't taken on the Moon.

B If you stood on the Moon at night and looked at the sky, would you see the stars? Explain your answer. (Level 4)

The scientists' answer is that the black sky fools people into thinking that the photo was taken at night.

In fact it was taken in the daytime and the Sun is shining on the astronauts' highly reflective white space suits. The camera's light levels were adjusted to show the astronauts clearly. The stars are in the sky but they do not glow brightly enough to be seen.

The phases of the Moon

The shape of the Moon seems to change each month because the Moon orbits the Earth once every 28 days. On day 1 there is a **New Moon**. The Moon is between the Sun and the Earth. The Earth faces the dark, unlit side of the Moon and the Moon is highest in the sky during the daytime. At this stage we are unlikely to see the Moon at all.

As the Moon orbits the Earth, we see more and more of the lit side of the Moon. After 14 days, the Moon is on the opposite side of the Earth from the Sun. We see a **Full Moon**. These changes are called the **phases of the Moon**. The diagram shows why the Moon appears to change shape as it orbits the Earth.

'I've been observing the Moon. Each month it seems to appear, grow and then disappear. But the Moon is always there, even though you can't see it.'

A time-lapse photo of the Moon ▲

The phases of the Moon ▼

day 7
day 11
day 4
day 14
Earth
day 1
light from the Sun
day 18
day 21
day 25

C How many days are there between each New Moon? (Level 5)

D Describe how and why the apparent shape of the Moon changes as it continues through its orbit to day 28. (Level 6)

day 1	day 4	day 7	day 11	day 14	day 18	day 21	day 25
New Moon		First Quarter		Full Moon		Last Quarter	

Keywords
Full Moon, New Moon, phases of the Moon

7.4 Winter and summer

Dawn in the coldest place on Earth ▲

Interesting fact

The coldest outside temperature on Earth was recorded in Antarctica in the winter. It was a bitterly cold –89 °C.

Imagine a place where it is dark outside for almost six months non-stop every year. Imagine how it feels to step outside and find darkness in the middle of the daytime. On Earth, there are two such places – the **North Pole** and the **South Pole**.

> **A** Where are the two places on Earth where it is dark continuously for nearly six months every year? (Level 3)

Why does this happen?

Jasmine and Ryan are having an argument. They have a lamp and a plastic ball on a skewer and are trying to work out why it's dark for so long at the South Pole.

'Perhaps in winter, the Earth stops spinning,' says Jasmine as she spins the ball.

'If the Earth stops spinning, everyone on this side of the planet would be in the dark for months and that doesn't happen,' replies Ryan.

'It's only the area around the South Pole that stays in darkness,' says Jasmine.

Ryan thinks. 'You have the ball spinning with the North Pole pointing straight up. What happens if you tip it over a bit?' he says.

Jasmine tips the ball over. 'It works!' she says. 'I've got the North Pole pointing towards the Sun and the South Pole is in shadow all the time.'

▲ Spinning the ball with its axis tilted

> **B** Draw a picture to show how the South Pole stays in darkness during its winter. (Level 4)

Why do we get seasons?

Jasmine and Ryan's idea fits the facts and agrees with what scientists say. The Earth's axis is tilted at an angle of 23°.

The idea that the Earth is spinning on a tilted axis explains some other things too. It explains the **seasons** and why we get more hours of daylight in Britain on a summer's day than on a winter's day. When the North Pole is facing towards the Sun, Britain spends more hours during each rotation in daylight.

▼ There are more hours of daylight during a summer's day than during a winter's day

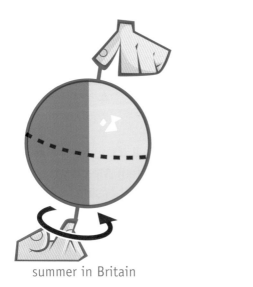

summer in Britain

winter in Britain

Six months later, the Earth is on the other side of the Sun. The North Pole is facing away from the Sun and Britain spends more than half of each rotation in the shadow. Use a lamp and globe to check it out for yourself.

C **Draw pictures to show why Britain is in darkness for longer on a winter's day than on a summer's day. (Level 5)**

D The axis of the planet Mars is tilted at 25°. The polar ice caps on Mars grow and shrink with a cycle of about two Earth years. Why do they do this? About how long is a Martian 'year'? (Level 6)

High and low

When you look at the Sun in summer, it seems high in the sky. This is because of the tilt of the Earth. In winter, the Sun looks lower in the sky. In summer, the high Sun shines directly on us, warming us up. In winter, the Sun warms us up less because the low Sun's rays are spread over a larger area.

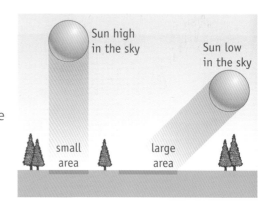

Sun high in the sky · Sun low in the sky · small area · large area

Keywords
North Pole, seasons, South Pole

7.5 Alien life

▲ Are these the faces of Year 7 on a planet many light years from here?

What are your chances of meeting an **alien**? Well, if you do, it's unlikely to come from one of the other planets in our **Solar System**. Mercury is totally dry and spins so slowly that one side bakes while the other side freezes. No life there.

Venus is covered in thick yellow poisonous clouds which trap heat. Any life would be fried. After the Earth, there's Mars. Mars possibly had water once but now it looks dry and dead. Further out, the outer planets are frozen and lifeless.

A Name four planets in our Solar System. (Level 3)

A new planet

▲ The new planet, Gleise 581c, might look like this

But astronomers think they've spotted a planet that may have life. This planet is not in our Solar System – it's 20 **light years** away. That means if an alien on the planet switched on a torch now, you wouldn't see the beam for 20 years.

B If we send a signal at the speed of light to the alien planet, how soon could we hope to get a reply? (Level 4)

Venus, with its hot, toxic atmosphere, is unsuitable for life ▼

Why might this planet have life?

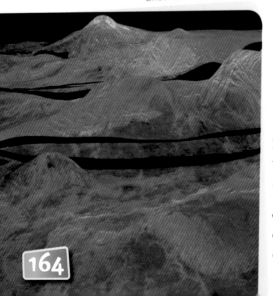

The new planet is in the 'Goldilocks zone' of its star. The story is that Goldilocks tried the first bowl of porridge and it was too hot. The second was too cold and the third was just right. The new planet is at just the right temperature to have liquid water.

Scientists believe that there must be water for life to begin, because they think life on Earth began in liquid water. The temperature of a planet depends on how far it is from its star.

- Some planets, like Venus, are too close and any water just boils away.
- Other planets, like Neptune, are too distant and any water is frozen solid.
- Planets in the Goldilocks zone are at the right distance for liquid water.

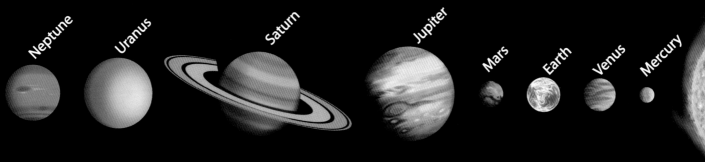

Neptune Uranus Saturn Jupiter Mars Earth Venus Mercury Sun

C Why can't planets outside the Goldilocks zone have alien life? (Level 5)

▲ The planets in our Solar System (not to scale). Earth is in the Goldilocks zone. Planets further out are too cold for liquid water

What is the new planet like?

Gleise 581c is more massive than the Earth, so it has more gravity. The more massive the planet, the stronger its gravity. If you went there, you would feel very heavy and walking would be hard work.

◄ Jupiter has twice the mass of all the other planets in our Solar System added together. On a massive planet like Jupiter, gravity is much stronger.

Aliens on a high-gravity ▶ planet would need to be strong and sturdy

D Would your mass be more or less on Jupiter than on Earth? Would your weight be more or less? (Level 6)

Making contact

Until there's a very fast way to travel, we can't visit the new planet. But we can send messages. Perhaps we'll hear back from beings like us who are intelligent and able to communicate. But perhaps we're trying to talk to a patch of slime growing on a rock!

Scientists at work

Spotting planets, especially small ones, around other stars is very hard. Astronomers don't know how many planets there are in our galaxy, but they guess there are billions.

Keywords
alien, light year, Solar System

7.6 Life, the Universe and what's outside

Learn about:
- why scientists sometimes change their ideas about the Universe
- some questions that scientists can't yet answer
- some questions that are not suited to scientific investigation

Planet Earth ▲

The Universe is gigantic. It contains billions and billions of stars separated by huge distances of almost empty space. It is only now, with telescopes, probes and space travel, that it's possible to see how very big the Universe is.

A Name three things that help scientists today to investigate space. (Level 3)

Interesting fact

There are many mysteries about our Universe – including whether it's the only one! Some scientists think there are billions of universes. Others believe there's just one.

Seeing is believing

We all, including scientists, form our ideas about the Universe on the basis of what we see and what we believe to be true. Now that astronomers have better telescopes, they've spotted things that have led them to change their ideas about the Universe.

▲ Your brain tries to make sense of what you see. This optical illusion gives confusing visual clues

B What leads scientists to change their ideas about the Universe? (Level 4)

Big questions

Did the Universe always exist?

Scientists say it started from a dot, long ago.

Then what was here before?

▲ Astronomers think the Universe began as a super-massive dot that grew amazingly rapidly. This is known as the 'Big Bang'

What came before?

According to the 'Big Bang' theory, space and time began when the Universe began. So if you want to know what existed before the Universe, then one answer is that there was no before.

Science can't answer every type of question. Science looks at how natural things work. It can give us clues about how the Universe began, but not whether everything is meant to be here or just happened.

Some people say that the Universe exists because there's a creator who planned it. Can science tell us if this is true?

C **Which of these claims is easier to test scientifically: 'it is always wrong to steal'; 'a silver wire is stronger than a gold wire'? Try to explain why. (Level 5)**

I don't think science can investigate that kind of question.

Inspiration strikes

Scientists have different views about why the Universe exists. One of the most famous scientists of all time, Isaac Newton, was a religious man who believed that a creator designed the Universe. This idea inspired him in his work.

There is a story that Newton sat under a tree, trying to work out why the Moon stays in its orbit and doesn't drift away through space. An apple fell down from a branch. Suddenly, Newton realised the answer. Gravity must work across space, as well as on the Earth. The Earth pulls apples and it also pulls the Moon. To Newton, it made perfect sense. Why would a cosmic designer invent two types of force when one would do?

▲ Isaac Newton

D Newton believed that the Universe must work as simply as possible. How did this approach help him work out which force holds the Moon in orbit? (Level 6)

7 Assess your progress

7.2 In a spin

1 Use the idea that the Earth rotates on its axis to explain why it is dark outside at night. (Level 3)

2 In science, a day is the time from one sunrise to the next. How many hours are there in a day? (Level 3)

3 Jupiter rotates once in about 10 hours. Is a day on Jupiter longer or shorter than a day on Earth? (Level 4)

4 People worked out that the Earth is spherical before they had space travel. Give one clue they might have seen to work this out. (Level 5)

5 If you travel from Britain to Australia, will you still see the same stars overhead? Explain your answer. (Level 6)

7.3 All about the Moon

1 How many days are there between one Full Moon and the next? (Level 3)

2 How much of its orbit does the Moon complete in one Earth day? (Level 3)

3 What does the Moon appear to look like 21 days after a New Moon? (Level 4)

4 Some planets have two moons. Would someone on the planet see both moons showing the same phase at the same time? Explain your answer (Level 5)

5 Does the grey landscape in the photograph of Buzz Aldrin on page 160 prove that Nasa faked the landing on the Moon in 1969? (Level 6)

7.4 Winter and summer

1 When it is summer in Britain, is the North Pole facing towards or away from the Sun? (Level 3)

2 Are there more hours of daylight during a summer's day or a winter's day in Britain? (Level 3)

3 When it is summer at the North Pole, what season is it at the South Pole? (Level 4)

4 About how many more hours of daylight are there during a summer's day than in a winter's day in Britain? (Hint: Think about what times it gets light and dark in summer, and in winter.) (Level 5)

5 In Britain in the summer, we see the sun rise and set during the day. How does the Sun seem to move in summer at the North Pole? (Level 6)

Chapter 6 questions
continued from page 155

7.5 Alien life

1 Which planet other than Earth in our Solar System might once have had liquid water? (Level 3)

2 Is the Earth a planet or a star? Is the Sun a planet or a star? (Level 3)

3 How does a planet's temperature depend on its distance from its star? (Level 4)

4 Give two reasons why scientists think that Venus cannot support life. (Level 5)

5 Explain how a planet's distance from its star affects its chances of having liquid water. (Level 6)

7.6 Life, the Universe and what's outside

1 What scientific instrument helps astronomers find out about the Solar System and the distant Universe? (Level 3)

2 Does science rule out the possibility of a creator? Explain your answer. (Level 5)

3 What do many scientists say about what, if anything, was around before the Universe began? (Level 5)

4 The strength of the force of gravity between two objects depends on the distance between them and their masses. Why does the Moon orbit the Earth, and not simply orbit the Sun on its own? (Level 6)

6.12 Circuits

1 What happens to the lamps in a series circuit of 20 lamps if one bulb blows? (Level 3)

2 What happens to the total resistance in a series circuit as more bulbs are added? (Level 3)

3 Use the model of current as water flowing in pipes to show that if one bulb blows in a series circuit, both bulbs go out. (Level 4)

4 Jasmine is making a model with two bulbs which she wants to glow brightly. Give **two** reasons why a parallel circuit would be a better design than a series circuit. (Level 5)

5 Copy out the final circuit in Amber's steady-hand toy on page 149. Explain how current moves round the circuit, using firstly the water model and then the cotton-wool ball model. (Level 6)

6.13 Lightning strike

1 How may volts does a D-type cell provide? (Level 3)

2 Can a lightning strike kill its victim? (Level 3)

3 Why is a shock from the mains power supply potentially fatal? (Level 4)

4 You are in a field in a lightning storm and your friend says 'Keep down low'. Is this good advice? Why or why not? (Level 5)

5 The BBC Weather site says you are more likely to be struck by lightning than to win the lottery. What does this tell you about the chances of winning the lottery? (Level 5)

A risky business

Learn about:
- the differences between hazards and risks
- how to recognise hazards in the science lab
- how you can control risks

Stay safe when you are doing experiments ▲

TOXIC

CORROSIVE

HARMFUL

IRRITANT

▲ Some hazard warning symbols

Carrying out experiments in your school science lab can be very exciting. They can be a fun way of learning new things about science. There are lots of different experiments. In chemistry, for example, you may do experiments where you have to add one chemical to another or heat up liquids using a Bunsen burner.

All these experiments are quite safe as long as you watch out for things that could go wrong and follow a few simple rules.

Hazards

A **hazard** is something that can cause harm. There are lots of different types of hazard that you might come across when you are working in the school lab. The table shows some of them and explains why they are hazards.

Hazard	Example	Why are they hazards?
chemical substances	acid	acid can burn you
biological materials	onion	onions can cause irritation to your eyes and nose
physical hazards	electrical equipment	electrical equipment can give you an electric shock
high temperatures	Bunsen burner flame	a Bunsen burner flame can set fire to your hair or clothes

▲ Some types of hazards

A Why is a Bunsen burner a hazard? (Level 3)

Rules in the lab

Your teacher will tell you the laboratory rules for your school. If you follow these rules you can avoid having accidents and you might be able to prevent other people having accidents too.

Here are some lab rules your teacher may tell you:

Lab rules
Don't enter the lab until the teacher gives you permission
Wear eye protection when the teacher tells you
Don't touch equipment unless the teacher says you can
Put your bag under the bench and keep the bench clean and tidy
Don't run in the lab
Report any spills or other accidents to the teacher
Don't eat or drink anything in the lab
Follow instructions carefully

B Explain why eye protection is important in a lab. (Level 4)

All about risks

A **risk** is the possibility of harm being done to you or someone else by a particular hazard. It is important for you to be able to identify hazards and then do something to reduce the risk of them causing harm. For example, if you cycle at night the hazard is not being seen by people in cars. The risk is the possibility that you might get run over. You can reduce the risk by wearing reflective clothing.

The picture shows some of the pupils of Class 7a, who are working in their school lab.

What hazards can you see? ▲

Identifying hazards and risks

Hazard	Risks – why is it dangerous?	What should be done to reduce the risks?
pupils running	they could trip over and hurt themselves	no running in the laboratory

C Copy the table above and fill in all the hazards that you can identify in the picture. You should be able to find at least ten. Then fill in why they are dangerous and what should be done to reduce the risks. (The first one has been filled in for you.) (Level 5)

Keywords
hazard, risk

D Explain the difference between a risk and a hazard. (Level 6)

Working like a scientist

Fewer fish, fewer herons? ▶

Learn about:
- how scientists design investigations
- some different types of variables
- how data can be presented

Science is all about investigating the world around us. So how do scientists decide what they are going to investigate?

Making observations

Pete is a biologist. Every day he walks past a lake. Lots of birds live there, including a large colony of herons. Usually Pete sees about twelve herons. One morning, Pete sees only nine herons. This seems odd, so he keeps a record of how many herons he sees each day for the next few months.

Pete's **observations** show him that the heron population is decreasing. He decides to carry out an investigation to find out why. Most scientific investigations start like this with someone making careful observations.

> **A** What observation makes Pete want to carry out an investigation? (Level 3)

Carrying out an investigation

Once a scientist has decided to investigate something, they need to think about how they carry out the investigation. This involves:

- deciding on the question they want to answer
- designing a safe investigation
- making a series of measurements and repeating them if they need to
- presenting data
- looking for patterns and measurements that do not fit the pattern
- making conclusions
- evaluating the investigation by looking at what could be done better.

> Herons eat fish. My idea is that the number of herons is going down because the number of fish is decreasing.

Pete decides to measure how many fish there are in one part of the lake. He takes a measurement from the same part of the lake every week and at the same time of day. This helps to make his investigation a fair test. The table shows some of his data – scientists often use tables to display their results.

Time	Date	Number of fish
Day 1	Monday 14th May	38
Day 2	Monday 21st May	37
Day 3	Monday 28th May	34
Day 4	Monday 4th June	36
Day 5	Monday 11th June	32
Day 6	Monday 18th June	30

▲ Pete's data

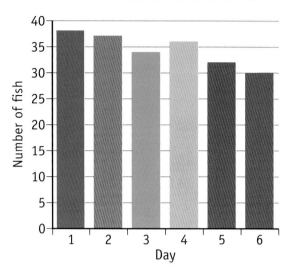

A variable is something that can be changed in an investigation to see what effect it has on the results. There are different types of variables.

- The time that Pete takes the measurement is the independent variable. This means that it is the variable that a scientist deliberately changes.
- The number of fish is the dependent variable because it changes as a result of changing the independent variable.
- The place where Pete takes the measurement and the time of day stay the same each time. These are called the **control variables**.

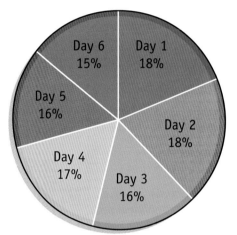

> **B** Which measurement was Pete's dependent variable? (Level 4)

Graphs and charts

Scientists can also use charts and graphs to display data. They have to be careful to choose the right kind of chart or graph as the wrong kind might not be helpful.

> **C** Which type of graph or chart is the best way of displaying Pete's data? Explain why. (Level 5)

What does the data show?

Scientists look for patterns in their data. One of Pete's measurements does not fit the pattern. There are more fish on 4th June than on 28th May. This is called an anomalous result. A scientist needs to decide whether an anomalous result is important or whether they can ignore it. Pete decides to ignore it.

Pete's conclusion is that the heron population is decreasing because the number of fish in the lake is decreasing. A **valid conclusion** is a conclusion that uses the data to support an idea.

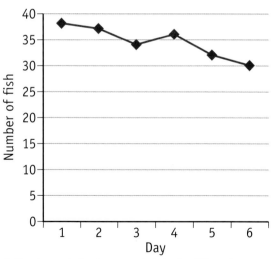

▲ Graphs and charts present data in different ways

> **D** Is Pete's conclusion a valid one? Can you suggest anything else that might be affecting the heron population? (Level 6)

Keywords
control variable,
observation,
valid conclusion

Glossary

acid A substance with a pH of less than 7. Weak acids taste sour, strong acids cause burns.

acid rain Rain polluted by acidic gases dissolved in it. Acid rain is more acidic than rainwater that is not polluted.

acidic Containing an acid and having a pH of less than 7.

adaptation A feature that helps a living thing to survive in a particular place.

adapted A well-adapted organism has features that help it to survive in a particular place.

adolescence The time in a young person's life when physical and emotional changes happen..

alien A life form that lives on another planet. Scientists have not yet found evidence of alien existence.

alkali A base that dissolves in water.

alkaline Containing an alkali and having a pH of more than 7.

ammeter An instrument that measures current in an electric circuit.

amniocentesis A procedure to remove some amniotic fluid from a pregnant woman's uterus that is then tested to check if the fetus has any genetic conditions.

amniotic fluid Liquid surrounding and protecting the developing fetus.

amphibian One of the groups of vertebrate animals. Amphibians lay eggs in water but breathe air. They have smooth, moist skin.

antacid Medicine that neutralises acid in the stomach.

atmosphere The layer of air that surrounds the Earth.

axis An imaginary line through the Earth from the North Pole to the South Pole. The Earth rotates around its axis.

balanced forces Forces that are equal in size but act in opposite directions.

base A substance that neutralises an acid.

battery More than one cell connected together in an electric circuit.

behaviour The way in which animals, including humans, respond to their environment, a situation, or other organisms.

binomial system A way of naming living things by giving them two Latin names.

biodome A closed artificial structure which plants and animals can live inside without help from humans.

biomass The total mass of living things in an environment. Biomass can be used as an energy resource.

bird One of the groups of vertebrate animals. Birds lay eggs with hard shells, look after their young and have feathers and wings.

black hole A dot in space that contains a huge amount of compressed matter. The force of gravity around a black hole is so strong that light is pulled into it.

boiling A liquid changes into a gas at its boiling point.

boiling point The temperature at which bubbles of vapour form throughout a liquid, not just from its surface.

braking distance The distance it takes to stop a vehicle after the brakes have been pressed.

camouflage Features that help something to blend in with its surroundings.

cancer A disease caused by cells multiplying out of control

carbon dioxide A gas that is produced when carbon burns and joins with oxygen, or when a carbonate reacts with an acid. Carbon dioxide turns limewater milky.

carbonate A substance that reacts with acid to produce carbon dioxide. Many rocks are made of carbonates.

carnivore An animal that feeds on other animals.

cell (in living things) A tiny building block that makes up all living things.

cell (in electric circuits) A device that contains stored chemical energy and converts it to electrical energy.

cell division When cells split to make more cells.

cell membrane A thin layer that surrounds the cell and controls the movement of substances in and out of the cell.

cell sap The liquid inside the vacuole of a plant cell.

cell theory The idea that all living things are made up of cells.

cell wall A tough box-like structure around plant cells.

cervix A ring of muscle at the opening of the uterus.

chemical energy Energy that is stored in a substance. It is transferred into other forms of energy during chemical reactions.

chemical reaction A change that makes a new substance.

chlorophyll A green substance that is needed for a plant to make its own food by photosynthesis.

chloroplast The part of the plant cell that contains chlorophyll and carries out photosynthesis.

chromatography A method used to separate mixtures of substances by their colour.

circulatory system An organ system that transports substances around the body.

classification Putting things with similar features into the same group.

coal A fuel made from plants that lived millions of years ago.

combustion The chemical reaction that happens when something burns.

concentrated A solution containing a lot of dissolved solute.

concrete A tough material made from sand, gravel and cement.

condensing Changing from a gas to liquid.

conservation Activities aimed at preserving the animals and plants living in a habitat.

conserved Neither lost nor gained, meaning that the same amount is present at the end as there was at the start.

consumer An animal that eats (consumes) plants or other animals.

contact force A force which needs objects to be in contact to affect them.

contraceptive pill A pill that prevents a woman from becoming pregnant.

contract To get smaller, when the particles making up something take up less room.

control variable A variable that is kept the same during an experiment or investigation.

corrosion Eating away of the surface of a solid by a chemical reaction.

corrosive A substance that attacks and destroys living tissue.

coverslip A very thin sheet of glass used to cover a sample on a microscope slide.

CO_2 emissions The amount of carbon dioxide a machine produces.

culture medium A special substance in which cells can grow.

current Electricity flowing around a circuit.

cutting A piece of a plant from which a new plant can be grown.

cytoplasm A jelly-like substance found inside cells.

dependent variable A variable that changes as a result of a change in an independent variable during an experiment or investigation.

diffusion Gas or liquid particles spreading out as their particles move and mix.

digest Process by which food is broken down into small pieces.

digestive system The organ system that breaks down your food into smaller pieces and absorbs them.

dilute A solution that does not contain very much dissolved solute.

diurnal Living things which are active during daylight and inactive at night.

dormant A state in which an organism is not active, allowing it to survive harsh conditions such as the winter.

Down's syndrome A genetic condition. People with Down's syndrome usually have learning difficulties and can have heart problems

egg A sex cell in a female animal. The egg joins with the male sex cell in reproduction.

electrical energy Energy carried by electricity.

embryo A tiny ball of cells formed from the fertilised egg when animals reproduce.

energy transfer The movement of energy from one place or form to another.

energy What makes things work. When anything happens, energy is transferred.

environment The surroundings in which plants or animals live.

environmental feature A condition in a habitat which affects what can survive there, such as temperature.

ethologist A scientist who studies animal behaviour.

ethology The study of animal behaviour.

evaporate Change from a liquid into a gas.

evaporating Changing from a liquid to a gas.

expand To get bigger. When the particles making up something take up more room.

eyepiece lens The lens of a microscope that is nearest to the eye.

feature A part of an organism, or a particular thing they do.

feeding relationship The link between predator and prey.

fertile Able to reproduce.

fertilisation In an animal, a sperm joining with an egg to make a baby. In a flowering plant, a pollen grain joining with an egg cell to make a seed.

fetus A developing baby inside the uterus of a female mammal.

filtrate The liquid that passes through filter paper during filtering.

fire triangle A way to show the three things needed for a fire to burn – fuel, oxygen and thermal energy.

fish One of the groups of vertebrate animals. Fish live in water and lay eggs there. They breathe through gills and have scales and fins.

flowering plant A plant that has flowers.

focusing knob The knob on a microscope that is turned to bring the image of the specimen into focus.

food chain A diagram that shows how the organisms in a habitat feed on each other.

food web Two or more food chains link together to form a food web, which shows the feeding relationships between the organisms.

force Something that causes an object to change speed, shape or direction.

fossil fuel Fuel made from the remains of animals and plants that lived millions of years ago.

freezing Changing from a liquid to a solid.

friction The force made when two objects rub together.

fuel A substance that transfers chemical energy to the environment as thermal energy and light energy when it burns.

fuel consumption The amount of fuel a car uses in a given distance, either a mile or a kilometre.

Full Moon The Moon with its bright side facing the Earth, fully lit by the Sun.

fuse A safety device for electric circuits. It has a very thin wire that is heated by current. If the current gets too high, the fuse melts and breaks the circuit.

gas A state of matter that is easily squashed. Its shape and volume can change.

gene An instruction that controls how an organism's features develop.

gland An organ that makes and releases chemicals such as hormones.

gravitational energy Energy stored in an object because it is off the ground.

gravity An attractive force between objects caused by their mass.

greenhouse effect The carbon dioxide in the air stops some of the heat energy escaping from the Earth, making the Earth warmer. It behaves like the glass in a greenhouse.

greenhouse gas A gas, such as carbon dioxide, that stops heat energy escaping from the Earth.

habitat The place where an organism lives.

harmful A substance that can make you ill if breathed in, swallowed or taken in through the skin.

hazard Something which can be a source of danger.

hazard warning sign A label containing pictures to warn you of the dangers of a chemical.

herbivore An animal that feeds on plants.

hibernate When an animal goes into a deep sleep to survive difficult conditions in the winter.

hormone A chemical messenger in the body that causes changes.

hydrogen An explosive gas.

identical twins Two babies, from a single fertilised egg, that develop together inside the mother and are born at the same time. They look very similar.

incubator A machine used in hospitals to keep premature babies alive.

independent variable A variable that a scientist deliberately changes during an experiment or investigation.

indicator A substance that changes colour depending on whether it is in an acidic, neutral or alkaline solution.

indigestion Pain in your stomach when you have problems digesting food.

infertility Not being able to reproduce naturally. If the man or woman is infertile, then the couple cannot have babies without treatment.

inherited Passed on from the parents to their offspring.

innate behaviour Behaviour which an animal has when it is born. It is also called instinctive behaviour.

input variable A variable that you change in an experiment. It is also called an independent variable.

insoluble Not dissolving in a solvent.

instinctive behaviour Behaviour which an animal has when it is born. It is also called innate behaviour.

interdependent Organisms in the same food chain all depend on each other.

invertebrate An animal without a backbone or a bony skeleton.

irreversible Something that cannot be changed back to how it was before.

irritant A substance that can cause red or blistered skin.

IVF Artificial fertilisation outside the female's body.

joule Energy is measured in joules.

kilogram Mass is measured in kilograms.

kinetic energy The scientific name for movement energy.

kingdom The largest group used in classification, such as the plant or animal kingdom.

learned behaviour A behaviour that an animal learns how to do.

light energy Energy transferred by light.

light year The distance that a beam of light travels in one year. It is used to describe huge distances in space. A light year is about 10,000,000,000,000 km.

limescale A hard white substance which is mostly made of calcium carbonate.

limewater A solution used to test for carbon dioxide. Limewater turns milky when carbon dioxide bubbles through it.

liquid A state of matter that flows. It can change its shape but it has a fixed volume.

litmus An indicator that turns red in acids and blue in alkalis.

lunar eclipse An eclipse that occurs when the Moon moves into the Earth's shadow. The Moon looks very dark.

magnetism A non-contact force that can affect some atoms, such as iron and steel.

magnification The number of times the image is made bigger by a microscope or magnifying glass.

mammal One of the groups of vertebrate animals. Mammals have hairy skin. Their babies develop inside the mother and are fed on milk.

mass A measure of how much matter an object has.

melting Changing from a solid to a liquid.

melting point The temperature at which a solid changes into a liquid.

menstrual cycle A monthly cycle in women. During the cycle, an egg is released and the woman has a period.

menstruation Part of a woman's menstrual cycle. The lining of the uterus breaks down and leaves the body through the vagina.

migrate Some animals, including many birds, move to a different habitat to avoid difficult conditions.

model An idea used by scientists to explain something that cannot be seen.

monotreme A type of mammal which has features in common with other mammals, but also lays eggs. There are only two types of monotreme: the echidna and the platypus.

natural gas A gas made from animals that lived millions of years ago. It is commonly used as a fuel for heating homes and for generating electricity.

nervous system An organ system that carries information around the body.

neutral A substance that is not acidic or alkaline, and has a pH of 7.

neutralisation The reaction between an acid and a base.

newton Force is measured in newtons.

New Moon We see a New Moon when the Moon is between the Sun and the Earth. There is no light from the Sun shining on the side we see from Earth.

nocturnal Living things which are inactive during daylight and active at night.

non-flowering plant A plant which does not have flowers.

non-identical twins Two babies born from the same mother at the same time from different sperm and eggs. Unlike identical twins, they look different.

non-renewable energy An energy resource that is not replaced as we use it.

North Pole The northern end of the Earth's axis.

nuclear A type of energy that most commonly comes from a radioactive metal called uranium.

nucleus The part of the cell that controls everything the cell does.

observation Something which is noticed and recorded during an experiment or investigation.

oestrogen A female sex hormone.

oil A liquid fuel made from animals that lived millions of years ago.

omnivore An animal that feeds on both plants and animals.

organ A group of tissues that work together to carry out a particular function.

organ transplant An operation in which an organ from a healthy person is put into a patient to replace a damaged organ.

organ system A collection of organs that work together for a particular function.

output variable The variable that changes during an experiment. The output variable is the thing you measure.

ovary In an animal, part of the female reproductive system that makes eggs. In a plant, part of the flower that makes the egg cells.

oviduct A tube in the female reproductive system that carries eggs from the ovary to the uterus.

ovulation When an egg is released from an ovary into an oviduct.

oxygen A gas found in air. It is needed for respiration and combustion.

parallel circuit A circuit that has more than one loop.

particle A tiny part that makes up every type of substance.

penis The part of the male reproductive system that allows sperm to be placed inside the vagina.

period Part of a woman's menstrual cycle. The lining of the uterus breaks down and leaves the body through the vagina.

pH scale A number scale that measures the strength of acidity and alkalinity.

phases of the Moon The different shapes of the Moon we see as it orbits the Earth.

physical change A change that does not involve a new substance being produced. A physical change can be reversed.

phytoplankton Tiny plants that live in seawater.

placenta Structure formed in a pregnant, female mammal. The developing baby gets its food and oxygen through the placenta.

planet A ball of matter in space that orbits around a star. The Earth is a planet.

potential energy The scientific name for stored energy.

predator An animal that hunts and eats other animals.

premature A baby born before the end of the normal pregnancy period.

prey An animal that is hunted and eaten by a predator.

producer A plant that makes its own food by converting light energy.

product A new substance that is made in a chemical reaction.

puberty The physical changes that happen at the beginning of adolescence.

reactant A substance that takes part in a chemical reaction.

relationship A pattern that links variables together. A relationship describes how the output variable changes when the input variable is changed.

renewable energy An energy resource that can be replaced as we use it.

reproductive system All of the organs used in the process of reproduction.

reptile One of the groups of vertebrate animals. Reptiles breathe air and lay eggs on land. They have dry, scaly skin.

residue The solid that stays behind on the filter paper during filtering.

resistance A measure of how much a material resists the flow of electric current.

respiratory system An organ system that takes oxygen into the blood and gets rid of carbon dioxide.

reversible Something that can be changed back to how it was before.

risk The possibility of a hazard causing harm.

rock salt A mixture of sand and salt mined from under the ground.

rotate When something turns round and round on its axis.

saturated When it is not possible to dissolve any more of a solute.

scrotum The bag of skin that holds the testes.

seasons Times of different climate during the year. In the UK we have four seasons – spring, summer, autumn and winter.

semen A mixture containing sperm.

series circuit A circuit that has only one loop. All the components of the circuit are on this loop.

sex cell A specialised cell used for sexual reproduction.

sexual intercourse The man's penis enters the woman's vagina, and sperm are released into the vagina.

signal Something that affects an animal and causes it to respond. It is also known as a stimulus.

slide A glass sheet that a specimen is put on, when looked at through a microscope.

solar cell A device that transfers light energy into electrical energy.

solar eclipse An eclipse that occurs when the Moon blocks the Sun's light from reaching the Earth. A shadow passes across the Earth.

solar energy Energy given out by the Sun.

Solar System The Sun and all the objects orbiting it, including the Earth and the other planets.

solid A state of matter that has a fixed shape and volume.

soluble Able to dissolve in a solvent.

solute A substance that dissolves to make a solution.

solution A mixture formed by a solute dissolved in a solvent.

solvent A liquid that substances dissolve in to make a solution.

sound energy Energy transferred by sound.

South Pole The southern end of the Earth's axis.

species A particular type of animal or plant. Members of the same species can reproduce to make more of their kind.

speed How fast something is moving.

sperm Male sex cells in an animal. The sperm joins with the egg in reproduction.

sperm tube Part of the male reproductive system that carries sperm from the testes to the penis.

star A ball of gas in space that produces its own heat and light.

state change Turning from one state into another, such as melting or evaporating.

state of matter Solid, liquid or gas.

steel A strong metal often used in buildings, ships and bridges.

stem cell A cell which has not yet become adapted to do a particular job and has the potential to become any other type of cell.

sterile Unable to reproduce.

stimulus Something that affects an animal and causes it to respond. It is also known as a signal. The plural of stimulus is stimuli.

stopping distance The thinking distance plus the braking distance.

strain energy Energy stored in a material because its shape has been changed.

testis Part of the male reproductive system that makes sperm.

testosterone Male sex hormone.

thermal energy The scientific name for heat energy.

thinking distance The distance you travel when you are thinking about braking, before you apply the brakes.

tissue A group of similar cells that carry out the same function.

toxic A poisonous substance that can cause death.

umbilical cord Carries nutrients, oxygen, carbon dioxide and other waste substances between the placenta and growing fetus.

unbalanced forces Forces that are not equal in size and act in different directions.

Universal Indicator An indicator that changes between a range of colours depending on the pH.

uranium Radioactive metal fuel used to obtain nuclear energy.

uterus Part of the female reproductive system where the baby develops.

vacuole A bag inside plant cells that contains a liquid which keeps the cell firm.

vagina Tube-like opening to the female reproductive system. Sperm enter through it and the baby is born through it.

valid conclusion A statement at the end of an experiment or investigation about what has been found out, which answers the original question.

variable A thing that we change or that changes in an investigation.

vertebrate An animal with a backbone and a bony skeleton.

voltage The amount of energy stored in an electric cell.

wave turbine A device that transfers the movement (kinetic) energy of waves into electrical energy.

weight The force of gravity on an object gives it weight.

wind turbine A device that transfers the movement (kinetic) energy of the wind into electrical energy.

Index

Heinemann is an imprint of Pearson Education Limited, a company incorporated in England and Wales, having its registered office: Edinburgh Gate, Harlow, Essex, CM20 2JE. Registered company number 872 828.

www.heinemann.co.uk

Heinemann is a registered trademark of Pearson Education Limited

Text © Pearson Education Limited 2008

First published 2008

12 11 10 09 08
10 9 8 7 6 5 4 3 2

British Library Cataloguing in Publication Data is available from the British Library on request.

ISBN 978 0 435503 68 0

Consulting editors: Carol Chapman, Head of Science Selly Park Community College for Girls, Sunetra Berry, National Strategy Secondary Science Consultant

Designed and cover design by Nikki Kenwood

Typeset by Kamae Design, Oxford

Original illustrations © Pearson Education Limited 2008

Illustrated by Ron Dixon, Dylan Gibson, Andrew Painter, Kamae Design

Picture research by Bea Ray and Maria Joannou

Cover photo/illustration by Skwak © Pearson Education Limited 2008

Printed in China by South China Printing Company

We endeavor to ensure that the paper and board used in our books has been made from pulp sourced from sustainable forests. We are also dedicated to working with printers who meet the highest environmental and employment standards.

Acknowledgements

We would like to thank Abbeyfield School, Bartley Green Technical College, Chilwell Comprehensive School, Crypt School, Holy Trinity RC School, Market Bosworth High School, Tettenhall College for their invaluable help in the development and trialling of this course.

The authors and publisher would like to thank the following individuals and organisations for permission to reproduce photographs:

Page vi, **T** ©CSIRO, **B** ©Science Photo Library/Claude Nuridsany & Marie Perennou; vii, **T** ©Paul Ouboter/Conservation.org, **B** ©Corbis/Eric Nguyen; viii, **T** ©PA Photos/Tony Marshall/EMPICS Sport, **M** ©Getty Images/AFP, **B** ©PA Photos/Danny Johnston/AP; p ix, **T** ©Getty Images/Uppercut Images, **B** ©Corbis/Michael Prince; 2 and 3, ©Professors P.M. Motta & S. Correr/Science Photo Library; 3, **bottom, from L to R** ©Photos.com, ©istockphoto, ©Science Photo Library, ©istockphoto; 4, **T** ©Peter Gould/Pearson Education Ltd, **B** ©Getty Images/PhotoDisc; 5, ©iStockphoto/Elena Korenbaum; 6, ©Steve Gschmeissner/Science Photo Library; 8, **from L to R** ©Getty Images/PhotoDisc, ©Getty Images/PhotoDisc, ©Getty Images/PhotoDisc, ©Pearson Education Ltd. Studio 8. Clark Wiseman; 10, **T** ©iStockphoto/geopaul, **B** ©Susumu Nishinaga/Science Photo Library; 12, ©Alamy Images/Photofusion/Paul Doyle; 14, **T** ©Rex Features/Burger/Phanie, **B** ©Sidney Moulds/Science Photo Library; 15, **T** ©AP/PA Photos, **B** ©iStockphoto/Jayson Punwani; 16, ©Richard Smith; 17, **T** ©istockphoto, **BL** ©Pearson Education Ltd/Tudor Photography, **BM** ©istockphoto/Catman73, **BR** ©Photos.com; 18, **L** ©John Greim/Science Photo Library; **M** ©Science Photo Library, **R** ©Thomas Hollyman/Science Photo Library; 19, **T** ©Dennis Kunkel/PhotolibraryGroup, **M** ©microscan/PhotolibraryGroup, **B** ©iStockphoto/Andreas Reh; 20, **T** ©Digital Stock, **M** ©Rex Features/Sipa Press; 22, ©iStockphoto/Anne Clark; 23, **T** © iStockphoto, **B** ©Corbis; 24, ©iStockphoto/Kenneth C. Zirkel; 25, **T** ©iStockphoto/Tomasz Markowski, **B** ©Corbis; 26, ©iStockphoto/Chris Schmidt; 28, ©iStockphoto/Chris Fourie; 29, ©NHPA/George Bernard; 32 and 33, ©Mehau Kulyk/Science Photo Library; 33, bottom, **from L to R** ©Pearson Education Ltd./Tudor Photography, ©Corbis/Peter Endig, ©istockphoto, ©istockphoto; 34, **T** ©Reuters/Seth Wenig, **B** ©iStockphoto/Michael Svoboda; 35, **T** ©iStockphoto/Mark Kalkwarf, **B** ©FLPA/Gerard Lacz; 36, **top, from L to R** ©iStockphoto/Yong Hian Lim, ©Corbis, ©M.I. Walker/Science Photo Library, ©Getty Images/Digital Vision, **B** ©Getty Images/Digital Vision; 38, ©Alamy Images/ Suzy Bennett; 39, top, **from L to R** ©Corbis, ©Getty Images/PhotoDisc, ©Getty Images/Digital Vision, ©iStockphoto/Dan Schmitt, ©Getty Images/PhotoDisc, ©Steve Gschmeissner/Science Photo Library, ©iStockphoto/Christian Riedel, ©iStockphoto/cre8tive_studios; 40, ©AUS. Reed International Books Australia Pty. Lindsay Edwards Photography. With thanks to Lord Smith Animal Hospital, North Melbourne, Victoria; 41, **TL** ©iStockphoto/Gloria-Leigh Logan, **TR** ©Corbis/Martin Harvey, **B** ©istockphoto; 42, top, **from L to R** ©iStockphoto/Simon Parker, ©Pearson Education Ltd/Peter Evans, ©iStockphoto/Jane Brennecker, ©iStockphoto/Bart Broek; **B** ©iStockphoto/Sue Loader; 43, **from L to R** ©iStockphoto/ray roper, ©iStockphoto/Lisa Thornberg, ©Jim Allan/Alamy, ©photolilbrary/Mel Watson, ©Lawrence Stepanowicz/Alamy, ©iStockphoto/Moon Tears; 44, **T** ©PA Photos/Peter Brown/University of New England,

B ©iStockphoto/WinterWitch; 45, **T** ©Martyn Evans/Alamy, **B** ©Getty Images/PhotoDisc; 46 and 47, ©Digital Vision; 47, **bottom, from L to R** ©Jack Picone/Alamy, ©Visual&Written SL/Alamy, ©Pearson Education Ltd/Debra Weatherley, ©iStockphoto/Gord Horne; 48, **T** ©Science Photo Library/Louise Murray, **BL** ©NHPA/Bryan & Cherry Alexander, **BR** ©Corbis; 49, **T** ©Louise Murray/Science Photo Library, **B** ©Jupiterimages Corporation; 50, **TL** ©iStockphoto/Lawrence Sawyer, **TR** ©FLPA/Hugh Clark, **B** ©iStockPhotos/Nico Smit; 51, ©iStockphoto/Steven Love; 52, **TL** ©iStockphoto/Joann Snover, **TR** ©iStockphoto/Pattie Steib, **B** ©iStockphoto/Renars Jurkovskis; 53, **T** ©iStockphoto/Daniel Thomson; **B** ©Corbis; 54, **T** ©iStockphoto/Richard Clarke, **M** ©iStockphoto/Ksenia Kozlovskaya, **BL** ©iStockphoto/Martin Valigursky, **BR** ©iStockphoto/Dirk Freder; 55, ©Science Photo Library; 56, **T** ©Digital Vision, **B** ©Jupiterimages Corporation; 57, **TR** ©Pearson Education Ltd/Peter Evans, **L** ©Maximilian Weinzierl/Alamy, **BR** ©Jonathan Plant/Alamy; 58, ©Jeff Rotman/Alamy; 60, ©Lisa Eastman/iStockPhoto; 61, ©Robert Clay/Alamy; 66 and 67, ©louise murray/Alamy; 67, **bottom, from L to R** ©National Geophysical Data Center/R.T. Holcomb, Hawaii Volcano Observatory, ©U.S. Geological Survey, ©iStockphoto/Jason Lugo, ©Dr P. Marazzi/Science Photo Library, ©Pearson Education Ltd/Tudor Photography; 68, **T** ©istockphoto/Lidian Neeleman, **BL** ©Roger Scruton; **BR** ©Source Unknown; 69, **T** ©Pearson Education Ltd/Trevor Clifford, **M** © Pearson Education Ltd./Trevor Clifford, **B** ©Pearson Education Ltd/Trevor Clifford; 70, **T** ©Rob Broek/iStockPhoto, **B** ©Alexis Rosenfeld/Science Photo Library; 71, **T** ©PhotoDisc/John A. Rizzo, **B** ©Paul Morton/iStockPhoto; 72, **T** ©istockphoto/Christian Lagereek, **B** ©istockphoto/Nicolette Neish; 73, ©Corbis; 76, **T** ©istockphoto/Monika Adamczyk, **B** ©Peter Gould; 77, ©Getty Images/PhotoDisc; 78, **T** ©istockphoto/Rafal Zdeb, **B** ©istockphoto/Paul Vasarhelyi; 79, ©istockphoto/Thomas Pullicino, **B** ©istockphoto/Daniel Cooper; 80, **T** ©Victor De Schwanberg/Science Photo Library, **B** ©istockphoto/Sean Locke; 81, **all four** ©Andrew Lambert; 82, ©Getty Images/PhotoDisc; 83, **T** ©Mark Burnett/Science Photo Library; **M** ©Getty Images/PhotoDisc, **BL** ©Peter Gould, **BR** ©Peter Gould; 84, ©Jim Amos/Science Photo Library; 85, ©Corbis; 86, ©Corbis; 87, ©Philippe Plailly / Science Photo Library; 90 and 91, ©Getty Images; 91, **from L to R** ©Dr P. Marazzi/Science Photo Library, ©istockphoto/Oliver Sun Kim, ©Pearson Education Ltd/Debbie Rowe, ©Creatas; 92, ©photolibrary/Alexandre; 93, **T** ©Western Ophthalmic Hospital/Science Photo Library; **B** ©Justin Kase/Alamy; 94, **T** ©istockphoto/Nancy Louie; **B** ©istockphoto/Matt Jeacock; 95, **T** ©AJ Photo/HOP Americain/Science Photo Library, **B** ©Andrew Linscott/Alamy; 96, ©Dr P. Marazzi/Science Photo Library; 97, **T** ©Andrew Lambert, **B** ©Pearson Education Ltd/Jules Selmes; 98, ©Jupiterimages Corporation; 99, ©Andrew Lambert; 100, **T** ©iStockphoto/Ana Blazic, **B** ©Pearson Education Ltd/Andrew Lambert; 101, ©Martin Shields/Alamy; 102, **T** ©Pearson Education Ltd/Tudor Photography, **B** ©Crown Copyright/Health & Safety Laboratory /Science Photo Library; 103, **T** ©PhotoDisc/Cole Publishing Group/Ed Carey, **B** ©Lawrence Migdale/Science Photo Library; 104, **T** ©Pearson Education Ltd, **B** ©Pearson Education Ltd/Andrew Lambert; 105, ©Martyn F. Chillmaid/Science Photo Library; 106, **T** ©iStockphoto/Paul Senyszyn, **B** ©Adam Woolfitt/Corbis; 107, **T** ©Pearson Education Ltd/Gareth Boden, **B** ©Corbis; 108, **T** ©Getty Images/PhotoDisc, **B** ©Science Photo Library; 109, ©Andrew Lambert Photography/Science Photo Library; 113, **from L to R** ©Rex Features/Norm Betts, ©Dreamstime, ©Anthony Blake Photo Library/Amos Schiliak, ©Corbis/Tim Wright; 114, ©NASA/John W. Young; 116, **T** ©Corbis/Tim de Waele, **B** ©istockphoto/Mark Poprocki; 117, **T** ©Corbis/Schlegelmilch, **B** ©iStockphoto. Michael Gomez; 118, ©Serious Wheels/Bugatti; 119, ©Corbis/Danny Lehman; 120, ©PA Photos/David Jones; 121, ©PA Photos/ Paul Faith; 123, ©Corbis; 126 and 127, ©Digital Stock; 127, **from L to R** ©Digital Vision, ©Corbis, ©Digital Vision, ©iStockphoto/lijlexmom; 128, **T** ©Andrew Holt/Alamy, **BL** ©AUS. Reed International Books Australia Pty Ltd. Lindsay Edwards Photography, **BR** ©Rich Clarkson/Corbis Sygma; 130, **T** ©Getty Images/PhotoDisc, **B** © Christian Liewig/Liewig Media Sports/Corbis; 132, **T** ©PhotoDisc, **B** © Digital Vision; 134, ©iStockphoto/Johann Helgason; 136, ©Brian A. Vikander/Corbis; 137, **T** ©Janine Wiedel Photolibrary/Alamy, **B** ©Citroen; 138, ©Pearson Education Ltd/Andrew Lambert; 140, ©iStockphoto/Cyrille Lips; 141, **T** ©Digital Vision, **B** ©iStockphoto/Svetlana Privezentseva; 143, **from L to R** ©PA Photos/Tina Fineberg, ©iStockphoto / mihaicalin, ©iStockphoto/Mageda Merbouh, ©Science Photo Library/M. English/Custom Medical Stock Photo; 144 **T** ©London Aquarium, **B** ©Science Museum/Science & Society Picture Library; 145 **T** ©Pearson Education Ltd/Tudor Photography, **M** ©Honda, **B** ©Photodisc; 146, **T** ©David Crossland/Alamy, **M** ©Pearson Education Ltd/Gareth Boden, **B** ©Harris Shiffman/iStockPhoto; 147, ©NASA Kennedy Space Center (NASA-KSC); 148, ©Bert de Ruiter/Alamy; 150, **T** ©Lars Lentz/iStock, **B** ©DK Limited/Corbis; 151, © ArkReligion.com/Alamy; 152, **L** ©Lora Clark/istockphoto, **R** ©Jonathan Hare; 156 and 157, ©Dreamstime, ©NASA; 157 **BL** ©istockphoto, **BM** ©NASA/ Human Space Flight, **BR** ©Maria Joannou; 158, **T** ©PhotoDisc. StockTrek, **B** ©Corbis; 160, **T** ©NASA, **B** ©PhotoDisc. StockTrek; 161, **T** ©John Sanford/Science Photo Library; 162, ©Corbis; 164, **T** ©NASA, **B** ©PhotoDisc. StockTrek; 165, **T** ©iStockphoto/George Argyropoulos, **B** ©PhotoDisc. StockTrek; 166, **T** ©PhotoDisc. StockTrek, **B** ©Science Photo Library/Laguna Design; 167, **T** ©iStockphoto/Björn Kindler, **B** ©Science Photo Library/Sheila Terry; 170, © Getty Images/Ableimages; 172, ©Georgette Douwma/Science Photo Library.

The authors and publisher would like to thank the following individuals and organisations for permission to reproduce copyright material:

Buglife – The Invertebrate Conservation Trust www.buglife.org.uk, p38, 39; Jennions, M.D. 1998. The effect of leg band symmetry on female-male association in zebra finches. Animal Behaviour 55, pp 61–67; With thanks to the Barn Owl Trust – www.barnowltrust.org.uk, p60, 61; Best lesson 3.5 based on a worksheet devised for the CREST Award scheme. CREST awards recognise creativity in science and technology projects and are run by the BA (British Association for the Advancement of Science) www.the-ba.net/crest.

Every effort has been made to contact copyright holders of material reproduced in this book. Any omissions will be rectified in subsequent printings if notice is given to the publishers.